The ABC's of Personal Finance

by John Charles Pool and Robert L. Frick

DURELL INSTITUTE OF MONETARY SCIENCE
Harry F. Byrd, Jr. School of Business
Shenandoah University

©1995 Durell Institute of Monetary Science
Harry F. Byrd, Jr. School of Business
Shenandoah University
1460 University Drive, Winchester, VA 22601-5195

ISBN 1-882505-04-2

Printed in the United States of America

Illustrations by Jorge Silva

Tables and charts by Design House, Winchester, VA

Produced by AAH Graphics (540) 933-6210

To Jordan and Max,
and to Amy and Hannah,
who, we hope,
will begin thinking about stuff like this
sooner than we did.

Acknowledgments

Putting a book together such as this one is in some ways more a question of orchestration than of the craft of writing. Many more people are involved than the authors.

First, we want to thank Elizabeth Racer, Director of the Durell Institute of Monetary Science, whose patience and vision has steered this series to new levels, project after project. Thanks also to our editor Kathryn Bryarly who, at the least, kept us on track, and the rest of the helpful staff of the Institute—especially Dianne Singer and Kathleen Smith who continue to perform logistical miracles. And finally, of course, we want to thank the late George Edward Durell whose benevolence and foresight made all this possible.

And special thanks to copy editors Jack Rosenberry of the Rochester, N.Y. *Democrat and Chronicle* and *Times-Union*, and to Melissa Rosenberry. Once again, their fine editing and comments saved us the embarrassment of overlooking the obvious. The manuscript was also reviewed by Dr. Ross M. LaRoe of Denison University who, as always, was extremely helpful.

Preface

The title of this book may say "Personal Finance" but what it really boils down to is two things: making plans and making choices. That sounds simple enough. But surprisingly, many people don't even know where their money goes, let alone how to plan for a prosperous and secure future, and make the correct choices to get there. Consider these surprising facts:

- Almost 40 million people in the United States—the richest country in the world—live below the poverty line.
- U.S. savings rate is among the lowest in the world, less than one-fourth that of Japan.
- Most people are unprepared for retirement.

How can you be sure you don't become one of the millions of financially unprepared Americans who go through life dealing with one financial crisis after another—living from paycheck to paycheck? As with many things in life, a little bit of study can go along away. In this case, it's the study of personal finance. That's where the *making plans* comes from.

As for the *making choices*, consider these questions: what should your career be? How much should you save? Where should you invest savings? How can you protect what you've earned? What effects do taxes and inflation have on your plans? What big expenses loom later in life that you need to plan for—now? By starting to deal with these questions today, you will take control of your financial future, so that you will have more, enjoy more, and also sleep better at night.

If personal finance is such an important topic, why isn't it something commonly discussed over the dinner table? For many reasons. First, for some of us, money wasn't a big issue until the last ten or so years because prosperity went along with being an American. But these days, it's not a given that everybody will do better than their parents did, because real wages (wages adjusted to take inflation into account) for the middle class haven't risen since 1973. That means personal finance and careful financial planning have become even more important than they used to be. That's one of the reasons we wrote this book and prepared a teaching kit and video to go along with it.

The other reason is that starting early to think about personal finance and the things that go along with it, such as education and career planning, is more important than it used to be. As recently as 25 years ago the typical American could graduate from high school, find a job in a factory, work there 40 years and retire comfortably. But, because of increasing competition from foreign producers and the increasing use of high level technology in the production process, those jobs are becoming scarce. In today's world, at least a college education is required to find a secure job, raise a family and retire comfortably.

Times have changed, and so has personal finance. This book attempts to address those issues in a simple, readable, and understandable way. And as with any book on this subject, it's simply a starting point. Real success comes from lifelong learning, discipline and some common sense.

J.C.P. and R.L.F.

Contents

CHAPTER 5

The ABC's
of
Personal
Finance

Chapter 1

GETTING
ORGANIZED

And youth, that's now so bravely spending,
will beg a penny by and by.
—Conrad Aiken

In this chapter, we will first need to get a feel for what personal finance means and how we set ourselves up for a secure financial future. We will then start building a financial plan by first finding out how much we're spending and where it's going. Then we'll look at saving and at using credit, and set some financial goals. The next step is to find out how we can close the gap between what we have and what we want. Finally, we'll look at some people and products that can help us along the way.

INTRODUCTION

Not long ago the investment brokerage house, Merrill Lynch, had an economist at Stanford University prepare a basic test on what people know about their own finances, and then gave the test to 1,000 Americans selected at random. Fewer than 1 in 5 were able to answer more than half of the questions correctly. Let's hope you weren't one of them, but if you were, keep reading.

BUILDING A "SAFE" FINANCIAL FUTURE

Although personal finance can be a complex and even mysterious subject, if you take it down to a personal level it's not hard to understand. All you have to do is think a little bit about your present personal financial situation—no matter how old you are—and then consider where you want

1

to be in the future. Financial planning becomes a matter of getting from here to there. And you *can* get there from here. All it takes is a little planning and a little patience. Although, granted, having money helps.

To help visualize what we mean by personal finance, consider something we're all familiar with: a safe. But instead of a simple safe made of steel, think of this safe as your financial picture, like the one shown at left.

Imagine that the bigger the safe, the more wealth you have. You want your safe to be big enough so you can buy a home, take the vacations you want, afford nice cars and pay for college educations for your kids. You want your safe to be secure, so if you lose your job or your health for a time, your family will not suffer financial hardship. You will find that your safe has some leaks that just can't be plugged, such as those represented by taxes and inflation, but you can prepare and plan for them. And ultimately you will want your safe to grow so big that you can retire with money to spare. To do this, you will need a steady stream of money flowing into your safe, and you will need to minimize the money flowing out.

Unfortunately, many of us have safes that look like the one shown on the right.

The money flowing into it is equaled or exceeded by the money flowing out. That means when you open the door and look inside, it's empty—or worse, there's an IOU indicating money owed. This safe represents people who have given up control of their finances, and who live from paycheck to paycheck. Rather than saving money and earning interest on that money, they spend more than they have. Consequently, some may have to borrow money to pay their bills, losing even more ground because of increased obligations to creditors.

START WITH A BUDGET

The first step in getting your finances in order is often the hardest because it involves coming face-to-face with your spending habits. This is never a pretty picture. When many of us need cash, it's usually off to the automatic teller machine (ATM), push a few buttons and out it comes. No money in the account right now? Charge it. Friends going out to dinner? Well, you're not planning anything; why not tag along? You may even pick up the check.

Obviously, all this spending adds up, but if you don't make a conscious effort to keep track of the spending yourself, you'll never be sure if what you're spending your money on is really what will bring you the most satisfaction in life—especially financial security. *The best way to keep track of your spending is to make a budget.* All you need is a piece of paper, a pencil and some information that's easy to collect. (Later you'll be shown how to do it an easier way: by computer.) If you use a checkbook and charge card for most of your spending, most of your work is already done for you—simply look in your checkbook and at your charge card account statements. If you don't use charge cards or a checkbook, then you'll need a notebook to record every time you spend money. If you usually get cash from a bank automated teller machine (for which you *may* have to pay a fee), remember to keep the stubs for a few months. For other miscellaneous expenses, carry a notebook around with you and jot them down. Now we're ready to find out where all that money goes. Chances are you'll be surprised how the small expenditures add up.

You should do your budget on a monthly basis because the majority of paychecks go to pay monthly bills. (If you don't get a paycheck yet, try very hard to imagine that you do.) When you first record your expenses for several months, separate them into categories. Add each category and divide by the number of months you have been keeping records to come up with an average. To determine what percentage of your total monthly expenses are devoted to each category, such as food or entertainment, divide each

FIGURE 1–3	**Basic Budget Example***		
EXPENSES			**PERCENT OF MONTHLY BUDGET**
AUTO:			
Fuel	$ 40		2%
Loan	$ 250		13%
Repairs	$ 20		1%
Auto Insurance	$ 20		1%
SUBTOTAL		$ 330	17%
MISC.			
Clothing	$ 120		6%
Credit Card	$ 150		8%
Eating Out	$ 140		7%
Groceries	$ 200		10%
Gifts	$ 120		6%
Entertainment	$ 100		5%
Rent	$ 500		25%
Recreation	$ 60		3%
SUBTOTAL		$1,390	70%
UTILITIES:			
Phone	$ 60		3%
Gas & Electric	$ 100		5%
Water	$ 20		1%
SUBTOTAL		$ 180	9%
TOTAL	**$1,900**		**96%**
Income	$ 2,000		
Income Minus Expenses	$ 100		
Annual Disposable Income	$ 1,200		

* Totals may not sum due to rounding.

category by the total spent for the month. In Figure 1-3 we see an example of a monthly budget for a single person.[1]

A household has to make payments for rent or a mortgage payment, for utilities such as electricity, water and telephone, for insurance, groceries and usually a car payment. Other items, such as taxes, are usually withheld from your paycheck. In the Basic Budget Example, when you add up all these expenses each month, they equal $1,900. To find out what's left over, (a figure called discretionary or disposable income) simply subtract these expenses from your monthly income after taxes and other deductions are taken out. Multiply that number by 12, and you have a rough estimate of your disposable income for the year. That's the important part—the amount you have some control over.

KEY CONCEPT

DISCRETIONARY INCOME IS THE AMOUNT
YOU HAVE LEFT OVER EACH MONTH,
AFTER YOU PAY THE BILLS FOR YOUR BASIC
NEEDS.

So, for example, if your monthly income is $2,000 and your expenses are $1,900, your monthly disposable income is $100. That means your *annual* disposable income is $1,200 ($100 times 12). The important point here is: **disposable income is the key to your financial future. By increasing it, investing it and managing it properly, you can meet your financial goals.**

Now suppose you want to increase your disposable income, which you are going to need to do if you want to get ahead. The first thing to do, once you have a budget set up, is to take a hard look at your expenses. Start with the biggest items first. Let's say it is rent. Assume you're spending $500 a month for a one-bedroom apartment. If you moved to a two-bedroom apartment for $700 dollars a month and split the rent with a roommate, you'd be saving $150 a month ($500 vs $350), or $1,800 a year. You've just increased your disposable income by 150 percent—from $1,200 to $3,000. Next, go down the list and determine which other expenses you can cut or even eliminate.

---

[1] A blank household budget form can be found at the end of this book, along with other useful financial planning forms.

FIGURE 1–4		**Revised Budget***	
EXPENSES			**PERCENT OF MONTHLY BUDGET**
AUTO:			
Fuel	$ 40		2%
Loan	$ 250		13%
Repairs	$ 20		1%
Auto Insurance	$ 20		1%
SUBTOTAL		$ 330	17%
MISC.			
Clothing	$ 120		6%
Credit Card	$ 150		8%
Eating Out	$ 60		3%
Groceries	$ 200		10%
Gifts	$ 120		6%
Entertainment	$ 100		5%
Rent	$ 350		18%
Recreation	$ 60		3%
SUBTOTAL		$1,160	59%
UTILITIES:			
Phone	$ 60		3%
Gas & Electric	$ 100		5%
Water	$ 20		1%
SUBTOTAL		$ 180	9%
TOTAL	**$ 1,670**		**85%**
Income	$ 2,000		
Income Minus Expenses	$ 330		
Annual Disposable Income	$ 3,960		

* Totals may not sum due to rounding.

The most important thing here is to keep in mind that the small expenses add up. For example, do you spend $4 on your lunch every day? By bringing your lunch to work you could save $20 a week, or about $1,000 a year. Don't go overboard here or you'll wind up living in a cave and wrestling small creatures of the forest for nuts and berries. The object is to get as much disposable income as possible, and still maintain a comfortable standard of living. When you've trimmed as much fat out of your budget as possible, make a new budget with spending limits in each category. (See Figure 1-4 for a sample revised budget with almost $4,000 in annual disposable income.) In future months, measure how well you do against your baseline budget. Don't be discouraged if you don't hit your goals immediately. Putting yourself on a budget is often like going on a diet—it requires some fundamental changes in your life and it often takes some time before you begin to see the results.

After you have revised your budget, look again at your overall financial picture—your financial safe. You'll see a big difference and you've just taken the first step to financial health.

CALCULATING YOUR NET WORTH

The best way to keep track of your financial progress and success is by calculating your net worth. To calculate your net worth, simply add up the value of things you *own* (assets), and subtract from it things you *owe* (debts or liabilities). Figure 1-6 is an example of a net worth statement.

Typically, your net worth is the sum of the value of personal assets such as your house, your car, any savings you have, the value of any stocks, bonds, mutual funds or other investments you have accumulated, money in a retirement fund, and anything else you own which has a value that can readily be turned into cash, less any debts on the assets—the things you already own.

FIGURE 1–6 **Net Worth Statement**	
ASSETS	
Bank Account	$5,000
Car	10,000
House	100,000
Retirement Savings	2,000
Personal Property	
Jewelry	2,000
Furniture	2,000
Clothing	1,500
Total	122,500
LIABILITIES	
Mortgage	90,000
Auto Loan	8,000
Credit Card	2,500
College Loan	25,000
Total	125,500
NET WORTH	**($3,000)**

By calculating your net worth, you make a "report card" that tracks how well you're doing accumulating wealth. It can even point to areas where you need work, such as too much debt. The goal here, of course, is to help you learn how to control your finances so you can increase your net worth every year. As you go through life, you should plan to increase your net worth at a steady pace in order to afford the big ticket items that come as you get older: perhaps a second car, a house, a boat, a trip around the world or retirement as a millionaire when you're 50. You can't get there unless you take control of your spending, which is another way of saying that you have to begin thinking about saving and what it means to your financial future.

SAVINGS

Americans, as a rule, aren't terrific savers. They save, on average, about 4 percent of their income after taxes. That's far less than Europeans, who generally save 10 to 15 percent. The Japanese save 16 percent. (See Figure 1-7.)

In the United States we have a forced savings retirement plan called the Social Security System with contributions automatically withheld from everyone's paycheck or paid directly to the government if you are self-employed. More about that later. But the important point for now is that

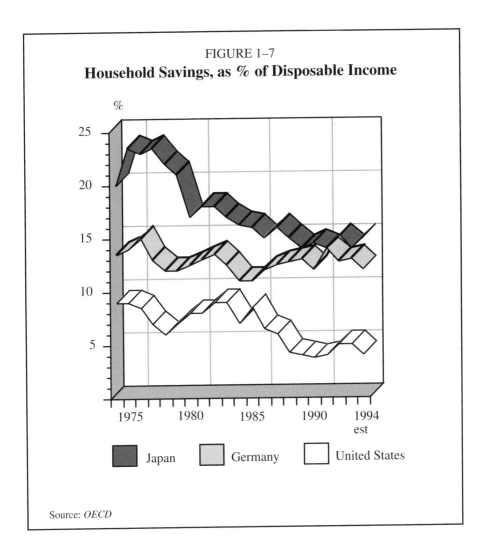

FIGURE 1–7

Household Savings, as % of Disposable Income

Source: *OECD*

many financial experts advise that you must save at least 10 percent of your pay just for retirement—in addition to Social Security. This doesn't take into consideration the savings needed to buy a house, send your kids to college or enhance your quality of life.

One reason Americans don't save any more than they do is because it costs more just to maintain the same standard of living that their parents had just a generation or two ago. After taking into account the effects of inflation, the average earning power of an American worker has dropped from about $8.55 an hour in 1973 to $7.39 an hour today, according to the Bureau of Labor Statistics. This means that even though the size of our paychecks may be bigger, the amount of goods and services we can buy with those paychecks has decreased. So not only does it **seem** that we're working as hard and getting less, we actually **are**. More on that later.

THINKING CLEARLY ABOUT SAVINGS

The easiest, most painless way of saving is by never seeing the money, which is easy if you have discretionary income, but not so easy if you don't. Your bank can help you establish a program which is right for you. For example, to make sure all your paycheck ends up in the bank, have the check sent directly from your employer to the bank. This is called direct deposit and many employers offer it. The check can go right into the checking account you use for monthly expenses. Next, have part of the check put into an account just for savings, using automatic transfer, without using credit cards or risking a bounced check. This method is often called paying yourself first because money goes to your savings account—and eventually to the purposes you want to use it for—before you have a chance to use that money frivolously. Even if it's not a large amount, you'll be surprised how fast it grows. So remember: *the trick to successful saving is to pay yourself first and remember that a few dollars here and there quickly add up.*

CREDIT

In the typical budget example, credit card payments of $150 a month were listed. That simple payment opens up a subject that is one of the most important keys to your personal finances: credit, which simply means borrowing money to buy something today that you will pay for in the future. Credit is a two-edged sword. When used properly, it can allow you great flexibility in managing your money and can even help you buy items that can add to your net worth, such as a house or a college education. When used incorrectly, credit burdens you with debt that makes you live in the financial past—paying off old bills, instead of saving for your future.

If you don't have a budget, you could end up going into debt, meaning you owe money to someone. For example, by borrowing money on a credit card, you end up paying interest on money owed, instead of collecting interest on money saved. How much of a difference can this make? Consider that a typical credit card balance can be $1,500. If the card charges 18 percent interest, you're paying $270 a year just in interest expenses! If you keep charging and making relatively small payments on your credit card balance—as many people do—at the end of the year you could still owe $1,500, and be $270 poorer. However, if you had saved that $1,500 instead of charging it, you could be making, say, 5 percent in interest at the bank, or $75 a year. The difference between spending and saving in this case would be $345 more in disposable income—$75 saved and $270 not spent in interest. Because of the high interest rates and sometimes low minimum monthly payments, credit card debt can seem to stretch on forever. For example, if you made the minimum payment on a $1,500 credit card balance—let's say about $40 a month, it would take four years and about $600 in interest payments to pay the bill off.

In general, as a rule of thumb, if your debt load is more than 15 percent of your take home pay, you are heading for trouble, if you're not already in it. To calculate your consumer debt load, add up all the monthly minimum payments you must make to pay off creditors (don't count a mortgage payment) and divide this by your monthly income, after taxes.

KEY CONCEPT

EXCESSIVE DEBT IS A BALL AND CHAIN
THAT KEEPS YOU FROM MOVING TOWARD
YOUR FINANCIAL GOALS.

Your ability to get credit depends on several factors, including your income and your credit rating. A credit rating shows how responsibly you have handled credit—meaning how faithfully you have paid your bills in the past—and is used as an indicator of how well you can handle more credit in the future. If your credit rating is poor, you can be denied credit when you need it, such as when you try to buy a car. Aside from not paying bills on time, writing checks on a bank account when you have no more funds in the account can hurt your credit rating, not to mention having to pay the bank a $10 or $15 fee on the bounced check, and sometimes having to pay a similar fee to the company you wrote the check to.

One of the first uses for your savings should be to pay off outstanding credit card balances. This is important for several reasons. First, you save interest charges. Second, if you work to keep your credit balances low, you remove the temptation to overspend. Finally, if your credit balance gets so large that you miss a payment, your credit rating is hurt.

If you don't have savings built up, then apply whatever you are saving out of your weekly paycheck toward your credit card balance. Also, shop around for a credit card with a lower interest rate, especially if you're going to be taking a while to pay off credit balances. Make sure you're paying 12 percent, or less, instead of 17 or 18 percent—the difference can amount to hundreds or even thousands of dollars in interest charges. To put that in perspective, remember that paying off the balance on an 18 percent credit card is the equivalent of getting 18 percent return on an investment or a savings account. Not a bad deal any way you look at it.

If you have several credit cards, consolidate the debt onto the card with the lowest rate, if possible, and cancel the others. Finally, if you feel credit is too much of a temptation, cut up your cards. You can always get new ones, but for now you'll be removing a temptation. If you want the convenience of a credit card without credit, many banks have cards that work like credit cards, except they take money directly out of your checking account.

Having said that (and presumably having done it), let's check back at your overall financial picture, as shown at right.

With expenses cut back, that big load of debt is reduced to a small one, or eliminated completely. And your financial picture is looking a lot better. Perhaps more importantly, you have taken control of your financial future.

SETTING GOALS

Now that you are on a budget, have gotten yourself out of debt, and have your bank accounts set up properly, what should you save for? First, most financial advisors recommend keeping between two and six months worth of your basic expenses readily accessible in case of emergency, such as losing your job. How many months' worth of expenses should you save? That depends on how risky you think your job is, how employable you are, how big your family is and how much debt you're carrying. You should keep your emergency money in a place where it is easy to get, such as a bank savings account or a money market fund.

That accomplished, and assuming you have an insurance plan in place (see Chapter 4 for more on this), now you can begin to set more interesting goals, which will become the road map for your financial future. To put that future into perspective, identify your goals and categorize them: short term, intermediate and long term. Short term goals are those that you should achieve in the next month, maybe saving enough to afford concert tickets or a short trip. Intermediate goals generally are those achieved within the next year, maybe for a vacation. Long term goals are those that are more than one year away. In the case of a teenager, a long term goal might be completing college or buying a house.

Remember that these goals need to be achievable ones—not just part of a wish list. For example, if you wish to go on a vacation this summer, you need to get an estimate of what the vacation will cost, the date you want to take your vacation, and a weekly or monthly amount you need to save to achieve the goal. Of course, you could always charge the vacation, but going into debt for such goodies is usually a bad idea. Months after your vacation is over and your tan has faded, you'll want pictures to remind you of your week in the Caribbean, not a stack of credit-card bills. Do not be afraid to look far into the future with your goals. As you will see in later chapters, in some ways goals that are many years away are more easily obtained—and with less savings than you might think.

Once you have a list of those goals, put a dollar amount on them. Let's say you want to save for a house down payment of $10,000, and you've managed to increase your disposable income to $5,000 a year. You could forego all luxuries, suspend all other plans and put every nickel toward that house down payment, and have it in two years. Or, you could use some of that disposable income for other things, and just put away $2,000 a year toward your house. That way, you'll have the down payment in five years.

By splitting your disposable income stream among the various financial goals, you can see which goals are obtainable and how fast you can get them.

Let's take a simple example, as shown in Figure 1-9. Assume you've just gotten out of college, are single, and will be saving $3,000 a year, which you'll split up to save toward different goals:

- You'll save $1,500 a year in a bank account at 5 percent interest for a down payment on a house, which you plan to buy in six years.

- You'll save $500 a year in a bank account for a trip to Europe in four years.

- After meeting your first two goals, you'll invest what's left over in the stock market (at a 12 percent return) for your retirement, which you'll use in 40 years.

In six years, you'll have more than $10,000 for a house down payment. In four years you'll have more than $2,200 for a trip to Europe. In 40 years you'll have $1.7 million for retirement. Wait a minute! How can $3,000 a year or less invested for 40 years add up to $1.7 million? Well, it's because of something called compound interest which will be discussed later. For now, keep in mind that: **LONG TERM GOALS ARE OFTEN EASIER TO REACH THAN SHORT TERM GOALS IF YOU PLAN SOON AND INVEST PRUDENTLY**.

When you do a budget and set goals, it's always a good idea to set aside some extra money to prepare for the unexpected. The furnace dies? Your luggage gets lost? Your tires need replacing? These little financial disasters can delay reaching your goals on time if you don't plan for them. You should also think of non-financial goals for your life as well, such as learning to play bass guitar or running a four-minute mile. Life isn't only about financial security and affording material things, after all.

KEEPING TRACK

When you start setting goals, remember to write them down and keep them somewhere within easy access so you can monitor your progress. A notebook or computer file will do. Your records don't have to be carved in stone. Write down when you hope to achieve each goal, and if it's a financial goal, how much you will have to save to achieve it. Most likely you will have to adjust your goals from time to time, as your financial situation and your personal desires change. Finally, if you imagine how good it will feel to reach those goals you will create a vision of future achievement, which can be a powerful motivator. Don't be stingy with your vision of the future.

FIGURE 1–9

Savings Plan

YEAR	ANNUAL SAVINGS	HOUSE	VACATION	RETIREMENT
1	$3,000	$ 1,500 *	$ 500 **	$ 1,000 ***
2	$3,000	$ 3,150	$1,050	$ 2,240
3	$3,000	$ 4,883	$1,628	$ 3,629
4	$3,000	$ 6,702	$2,234	$ 5,184
5	$3,000	$ 8,612		$ 7,486
6	$3,000	$10,617		$ 10,065
7	$3,000			$ 14,632
8	$3,000			$ 19,748
9	$3,000			$ 25,478
10	$3,000			$ 31,896
11	$3,000			$ 39,083
12	$3,000			$ 47,133
13	$3,000			$ 56,149
14	$3,000			$ 66,247
15	$3,000			$ 77,556
16	$3,000			$ 90,223
17	$3,000			$ 104,410
18	$3,000			$ 120,299
19	$3,000			$ 138,095
20	$3,000			$ 158,027
21	$3,000			$ 180,350
22	$3,000			$ 205,352
23	$3,000			$ 233,354
24	$3,000			$ 264,716
25	$3,000			$ 299,842
26	$3,000			$ 339,184
27	$3,000			$ 383,246
28	$3,000			$ 432,595
29	$3,000			$ 487,866
30	$3,000			$ 549,770
31	$3,000			$ 619,103
32	$3,000			$ 696,755
33	$3,000			$ 783,726
34	$3,000			$ 881,133
35	$3,000			$ 990,229
36	$3,000			$1,112,416
37	$3,000	* 5 percent interest		$1,249,266
38	$3,000	** 5 percent interest		$1,402,538
39	$3,000	*** 12 percent return		$1,574,203
40	$3,000			$1,766,467

FIGURE 1–10

Monthly Income and Expenses

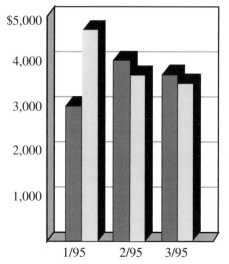

Expense Comparison as a
Percentage of Total Expenses

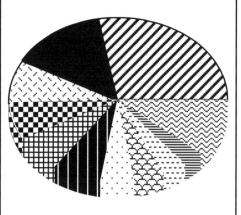

Mortgage	27.78	%
Groceries	14.21	
Utilities	8.58	
Clothing	7.47	
Miscellaneous	7.25	
Medical	7.10	
Insurance	5.07	
Expenses – Other	4.61	
Investment Exp.	3.57	
Gifts	3.02	
Other	11.33	
Total	100	%

> ## KEY CONCEPT
>
> TO ACHIEVE YOUR GOALS, YOU SHOULD
> WRITE THEM DOWN, ENVISION THEM AND
> CELEBRATE WHEN YOU REACH THEM.

You may be a person who does not have the patience to balance your checkbook, and sitting down every month to crunch these numbers can become a chore. Fortunately, computer software exists that make monitoring finances easy. Not only will these programs automatically add up expenses, they can match real expenses against your baseline budget, keep track of net worth and investments, calculate interest earned, help with taxes and even write checks and pay bills. Two such programs are *Quicken* and *Managing Your Money*. Many of the charts and examples used in this book come from these two programs (available most places where computer software is sold and sometimes even come pre-installed when you buy a computer). Figure 1-10 is an example of a family's expenses graphed as a pie chart from the *Quicken* program. Below is shown an example of the menu of features offered in the *Managing Your Money* program.

Source: *Managing Your Money*

GETTING HELP

Keeping track of your finances is only part of the battle. As you've seen so far (and which will become more evident in upcoming chapters), personal finance involves many different factors. Because of this, many people find that they need sound advice on such things as strategies, specific investments, and tax returns. There are many financial experts eagerly waiting to help you—for a fee, of course. Do you need help from experts? That depends on how much time you want to spend learning about personal finance and how much you're willing to pay someone else for help. If you do decide to seek advice, remember that the less you know about personal finance, the more vulnerable you are to receiving mediocre, or just plain lousy, advice from a financial professional. If you decide to turn your finances over completely to someone else, you're essentially giving up the combination to your financial safe. That's why it's important to know the basics, and why you want to seek out a professional who will not only give you advice, but will help educate you about finance. When seeking professional help, you need to keep two important things in mind: what qualifications do they have? How will they be paid?

Let's start by looking at the broadest type of financial professional, called financial planners. Financial planners are trained in a broad spectrum of investments, and can advise you on all your financial needs, such as insurance, budgeting and investing. However, anyone can be called a financial planner, just as anyone can be called a butcher or baker if they slice bologna or make cupcakes. So it's important to choose a financial planner with the best possible qualifications, preferably a certified financial planner, or CFP. A certified financial planner has at least three years' experience and has passed a test administered by the College for Financial Planners.

CFPs are likely to put you, as their client, through a six-step process designed to guide you on the road to financial security:

1. Gather personal and financial data.

2. Establish financial goals and objectives.

3. Process and analyze information.

4. Develop a comprehensive financial plan.

5. Implement the plan.

6. Monitor the plan.

A drawback to turning your financial affairs over to most financial planners is that their pay comes in the form of commissions. This means a percentage is paid to the financial planner on any products purchased such as insurance or a mutual fund. This percentage can be as little as 1 percent on an investment such as a mutual fund, to 100 percent of the first payment on a life insurance policy. Some say that working on commission creates a conflict of interest for the planners—their financial interests against your financial interest. Will they push you toward products with higher commissions so they can make more money? Or worse, will they have you buy and sell (trade) your financial products, such as stocks, too often? (This is called churning because each time you switch, they get a commission.) You want your financial planner looking out for your best interest, not theirs. Of course, most of them do.

> **KEY CONCEPT**
>
> PAYING COMMISSIONS TO FINANCIAL
> PLANNERS MAY CREATE CONFLICT
> BETWEEN YOUR INTERESTS AND THEIRS.

You can protect your interests in a couple of ways. First, you can be knowledgeable enough about personal finance and investments to monitor the advice the planner gives you, and know when you're not getting a good deal. Insist, for example, that all fees and commissions on products you buy through a planner be disclosed to you before a purchase is made. Second, you can seek planners who do not sell on commission, but are fee-based—meaning you pay them not by commissions, but by the hour, or according to the complexity of the financial plan—to come up with the best strategies for you. Some financial planners use both fees and commissions to earn a living. They may set a fee, then deduct the commissions they earn from selling you products from that fee. This helps prevent conflicts of interest. Sometimes the best advice from financial planners comes from those who work in a group practice, where different planners have different areas of expertise. This ensures that the help you're getting is thorough and up-to-date.

Another type of financial professional many people turn to is a certified public accountant or CPA. CPAs are usually knowledgeable about taxes, but may not have the training to deal with the financial big picture that financial planners do. Certified public accountants who also have had training in personal finance have the PFS, or personal financial specialist, designation. CPAs and PFSs usually are paid by fees, not commissions.

Insurance specialists also do financial planning, if they hold the chartered life underwriter (CLU) designation or the chartered financial consultant (CFC) designation. The thing to watch for from these planners is that they may recommend insurance products heavily—ones which may come with big commissions—when other investments may be more appropriate.

Likewise, you can receive financial advice from someone who sells stocks, bonds and mutual funds—commonly called a stockbroker, though many give themselves other titles these days. But just as with an insurance agent who sees every problem with an insurance solution, a broker may think only in terms of investments, and not give the broad-based help you need.

When looking for help from financial professionals, consider these qualifications and questions:

1. Do they come with a recommendation from someone you trust?

2. Do they have professional designations that show some level of competency?

3. How are they paid? Fees? Commissions? Some combination of the two?

4. Do they offer to tell you the commission they receive on a product before you ask? If getting that information is difficult, move on to someone else.

5. Will they tell you, up front, exactly what their advice will cost you in the first year and succeeding years?

6. Will they give you a financial plan in writing? If not, you are at a disadvantage because you can't take the plan home and study it at your leisure. Also, if you're buying a financial plan, you should have the option of implementing it yourself.

7. Do they speak in plain language? Some aspects of financial planning may be complex, but most of it can be explained in simple terms. If your planner uses financial jargon that is confusing, consider someone else—after all, part of what you're paying for is a better understanding of your finances.

LOOKING AHEAD

Now that we've started thinking in an organized manner about budgeting and financial planning, it's time to see if we can begin thinking more clearly about making money and using it to build a secure financial future. Then we'll look at how we can spend it to accomplish our goals.

Chapter 2

MAKING MONEY

He does not possess wealth that allows
it to possess him.
                    —Benjamin Franklin

In this chapter we look at how to think clearly about the payoffs
to education in your personal as well as your financial life. Career
planning is addressed and why it may be the most important
decision we ever make. Then, on the assumption that we are going
to make money if we make the right educational and career
choices, we take up the question of how to think about financial
success in terms of our allies: education, planning and time. We
will also examine our enemies: inflation, taxes and time. Note that
time is both our ally and our enemy, depending on how soon we
get started on a well-planned savings and investment program.

INTRODUCTION

When you get right down to it, making money boils down to four
things: planning, preparation, patience and persistence, the four "Ps" of success. Of course, luck often enters into the picture, but as a wise man once
said, "Luck is when opportunity meets with preparedness." That's why most
successful people don't succeed by accident; they spend a lot of time getting
prepared for it. The first step in that process is career planning.

CAREER PLANNING

Before beginning, you should remember that perhaps the most important part of planning a career and a successful financial life is to recognize
that you have some allies, if you choose to use them.

YOUR ALLIES ARE: EDUCATION, PLANNING, AND TIME.

Everyone wants to make money, and hopefully become rich. Money may not guarantee happiness, but it certainly helps. That leaves the question of how to become successful and have a secure financial life. The answer, of course, is careful career planning and a carefully thought-out educational program. The evidence is clear on one point: the more education you have, the more likely that you will earn more money and, at the same time, live a happier and more rewarding life.

Now let's look back at your "financial safe" that you are trying to fill up. Decreasing expenses and increasing saving, as you read in Chapter 1, is one method. But you want to make the money stream going into the safe as large as possible. (See figure 2-1, below.) Increasing this stream means

achieving your short-term and long-term financial goals more quickly. It means you can absorb setbacks more easily, and it means a higher standard of living.

For example, it's no secret that medical doctors and airline pilots earn a lot more money than janitors and truck drivers; indeed, they make two or three times more. A 1994 Census Bureau study showed that the average high school graduate can expect to earn $821,000 over the course of a working life (defined as working from age 25 to 64). That seems like a lot until you consider that the same study showed that a college graduate can expect to earn more than $1.4 million, or $621,000 more. And someone with a professional degree, such as a doctor or lawyer, can expect to earn more than $3 *million* over the course of a working life. That doesn't include the satisfaction of having a more interesting and satisfying job, and probably working indoors.

What's the deal here? Mostly it's education. No matter how you look at it: *education pays off, big time.*

Of course, that has always been true, but these days it is even more important than ever. As recently as the 1960s it was possible for someone to graduate from high school, find a job in an auto plant or some other kind of factory and earn a decent living—enough to buy a home and support a family—without the spouse having to work. But things have changed. Because of competition from lower-paid workers in other countries and a rapidly increasing level of technology, nearly all of those semi-skilled, relatively well-paying jobs have been eliminated as large corporations have been forced to reduce the number of workers they employ and replace them with computers and robots.

That has meant two things: one is that the average income of American households (when you take into account the effects of inflation) has not increased since 1973, even with both spouses now working in most house-

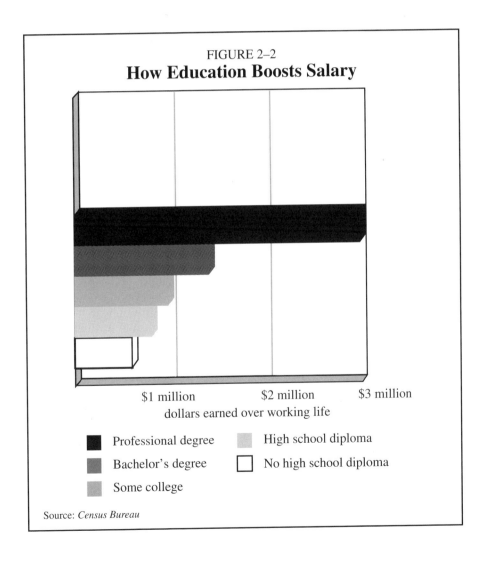

FIGURE 2–2
How Education Boosts Salary

$1 million $2 million $3 million
dollars earned over working life

■ Professional degree   ▨ High school diploma

▨ Bachelor's degree   ☐ No high school diploma

▨ Some college

Source: *Census Bureau*

holds—which was not common even 20 years ago. (See Figure 2-1.) Who has been hurt the most? Those with the least education.

The second thing is that in order to enter the work force now one has to be trained to use computers even in low level jobs. The new technological society, which functions in cyberspace, on electronic mail, and on the Internet makes a good education essential. Yet only 80 percent of Americans over age 25 have a high school education; only 22 percent have a college or post-graduate degree, and only 70 percent know how to use a computer. So if you want to function in this modern world and reap the rewards financial planning has to offer, clearly you need to think seriously about investing some of your time and effort toward getting an education. The payoffs are considerable, but the costs—though they may seem high at first—are, in reality, minimal.

One way to think about this is to think like an economist, which incidentally, is one of the higher paid occupations. An economist would tell you to think about education in terms of its **opportunity costs** versus its benefits.

KEY CONCEPT

OPPORTUNITY COSTS ARE THE VALUE OF WHAT YOU LOSE WHEN YOU CHOOSE ONE ALTERNATIVE RATHER THAN ANOTHER.

Nearly everything we do has opportunity costs. Even reading this book is costing something because you could be doing something else with your time, such as working. The choice to do anything involves the choice not to do something else. For example, suppose you decide to go to college. What does it cost you? Maybe $15,000 a year on average, covering the cost of your tuition, room and board, books, and transportation. Is that what it costs you to go to college? Your accountant may say so, but the economist would disagree. Why? Because you have to consider what you give up while you are in college. If you didn't go to college, but decided to work instead, you could make $8,840 a year if you earned the minimum wage of $4.25 an hour and got a paid vacation.[1] That $8,840 has to be added to the $15,000

---

[1] A quick and easy way to calculate your annual income is multiply your hourly wage by 2,000 which is roughly the average number of hours worked in year, not counting two

it costs you to go to college for a year because it's a foregone alternative; you could have worked instead. So, your total cost of going to college is $23,840 a year.

Now let's see if going to college is worth it. It costs you $60,000 to go for 4 years ($15,000 times 4), plus another $35,360 in lost income ($8,840 times 4) or almost $100,000 altogether. What do you gain? An extra income of more than $600,000 over your working life, for a $500,000 profit on the deal. Not a bad investment. But going to graduate school offers an even more dramatic example.

Suppose you have graduated from college and are considering spending two years earning a masters in business administration. The average college graduate gets a starting salary of around $25,000. The average MBA gets a starting salary of about $35,000. It costs, say, $20,000 a year to go to graduate school or $40,000 plus your opportunity cost of $50,000—roughly what you could have earned in those two years—for a total of $90,000. What do you gain? Starting at a salary $10,000 higher over an average working life of 40 years, you would earn $400,000 more, not counting the better opportunities for advancement and promotion having the MBA would probably give you. The net gain on that investment? A cool $310,000 plus a bigger office with a better view. The gains from higher level professional education are even greater, despite their higher cost. So to repeat, *any way you look at it education pays off*. You're probably convinced of that now, but you've still got the problem of choosing a career in a rapidly changing world.

CAREER CHOICES

There is a lot of information around about choosing a career, or starting a new one. But before you even think about that, you may want to consider what you want to do with the rest of your life, carefully thinking about what it is that you enjoy. Keep in mind that *money isn't everything*. If you think it is then you may want to consider going into business, which is where the money is, but is not necessarily where you find happiness. But, of course, some people enjoy the challenge of being in business for themselves or working in a business setting. Chances are if you enjoy competition and taking risks, business is the place for you.

---

weeks of vacation. So if someone offers you a job for $8.00 an hour, how much do you earn annually? About $16,000 ($8 times 2,000). That's something to keep in mind the next time you go on a job interview.

One way to tell is to get a job and see how you like it. Another is to begin reading business literature to see if it seems interesting to you. You might, for example, pick up a few copies of *The Wall Street Journal* and read them from cover to cover. If you find them interesting, you may want to consider business as a career. If you don't, you should think about a different choice, one that you will enjoy more. If you enjoy your work, the money will follow. If it doesn't, at least you'll still be happy, although not very well off.

Interestingly, many of the better jobs these days are not in business, but in the service industries. The U.S. government's Bureau of Labor Statistics, which tracks job outlook information through the Office of Employment Projections, estimates that almost all of the new jobs created through the year 2005 will be in the service sector of the economy. In fact, one out

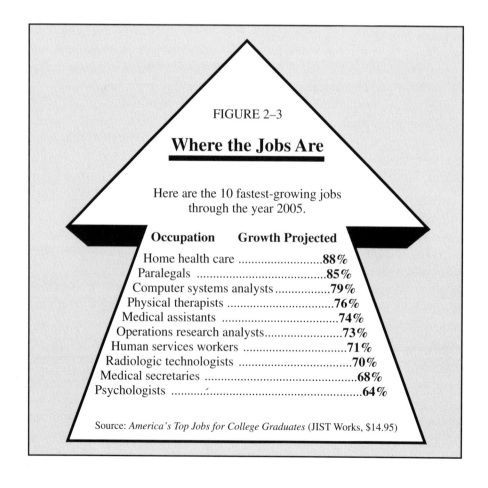

FIGURE 2–3

Where the Jobs Are

Here are the 10 fastest-growing jobs
through the year 2005.

Occupation	Growth Projected
Home health care	88%
Paralegals	85%
Computer systems analysts	79%
Physical therapists	76%
Medical assistants	74%
Operations research analysts	73%
Human services workers	71%
Radiologic technologists	70%
Medical secretaries	68%
Psychologists	64%

Source: *America's Top Jobs for College Graduates* (JIST Works, $14.95)

of every three jobs will be in the health field; almost as many will be in computer-related fields. Figure 2-3 breaks this down in more detail. Note that most of the fastest growing job opportunities are in the health sector.

Beyond that, check out a counseling center or your state or local employment office. A lot of information is available, and it doesn't cost anything except the opportunity cost of your time, which isn't much if you are in school, or unemployed. You'll probably find some helpful books in your library, such as the *Occupational Outlook Handbook* and *Planning Your Career*. And if you know how to use a computer (if you don't, that's the place to start), the best source is probably *Guidance Information Systems*, which is a computer program that cross-references careers with colleges that provide training for them and gives projections of future earnings probabilities.

But most important of all is getting some experience. If you think you want to be lawyer, get a summer job or an internship in a law office, where you can see and feel what goes on. As you watch lawyers go about their business, you'll be able to tell if that's the career for you and plan accordingly. The same applies, of course, for any career. You won't know if it's for you until you experience it. Alas, that's true for most things in life.

THE BIG PICTURE

Now that you've looked at the details of the prerequisites for making money and perhaps finding happiness as well, it's time to look at the larger picture. If you want to plan for a successful financial life there are some important things to keep in mind, no matter what career path you have chosen or how much money you make. Do you recall that at the beginning of this chapter you read that your allies are *education, planning and time*? Well, you also have enemies that can take the wind out of your sails no matter how good a navigator you are.

YOUR ENEMIES ARE: INFLATION, TAXES AND TIME.

Let's consider these one at a time and see how they fit into the overall scheme of things. Inflation is perhaps the most serious problem because it can erode even the best laid financial plan. Taxes are a necessary evil, which have to be paid. But that doesn't mean you have pay more than you have to. Time, as you will see, is both a friend and an enemy. It is, as John Randolph said, "at once the most valuable and the most perishable of all our possessions." Let's look at inflation first.

INFLATION

What is inflation? Inflation occurs when the price of the same good or service increases over time. Is that a problem? In many polls over the years the American public has indicated it considers inflation one of its biggest concerns. While inflation can be a serious problem if it gets out of hand—as it has a number of times in many countries—many economists feel the concern over inflation in the United States is somewhat misunderstood. In a simple sense, inflation is not a problem unless it reduces purchasing power—the amount of things you can buy with a given amount of money. That only happens when prices increase faster than wages, and that has seldom occurred in U.S. history, until recently.

```
--------------------------------------------------------
                     KEY CONCEPT
      INFLATION OCCURS WHEN THE PRICES OF
      THE SAME GOODS OR SERVICES INCREASE
       OVER A GIVEN TIME PERIOD, REDUCING
        THE PURCHASING POWER OF MONEY.
--------------------------------------------------------
```

To understand this, think for a moment what would happen if prices doubled while your wages stayed the same. Clearly you would be in serious trouble because the purchasing power of your income would be cut by half. But if your income also doubles when prices double, you are no worse off—and no better off—than you were before. Your *real wage*, meaning your actual wage compared to the rate of inflation, has stayed the same. So it is real wages that count, not actual (also called nominal) increases in prices.

```
--------------------------------------------------------
                     KEY CONCEPT
       REAL WAGES ARE CURRENT WAGES AFTER
             ADJUSTING FOR INFLATION.
--------------------------------------------------------
```

Over the years wages have tended to move with prices. Consequently, real purchasing power on average remained relatively constant until 1973, when real wages peaked. Since then, real wages of the average American worker have not increased significantly because the rate of wage increases and the rate of inflation have been almost equal. Put differently, while everyone seems to be making more than they were in 1973, the real purchasing power of their income now is about the same as it was then, hence standards of living have not increased much, if any.

The Incidence of Inflation

But there's more to inflation than that. One of the more important aspects of inflation is that it doesn't affect everyone in the same way. If you are a student, increases in the price of new homes or luxury automobiles won't affect your budget by very much, if at all. If you are retired, your spending is likely to be much different than that of a young couple just starting a career and a family, as they need to purchase a home, furniture and appliances. So price changes affect people quite differently, depending on their age, their needs, and their spending patterns.

But in one sense inflation can be your friend, depending on whether you are a debtor or a creditor. If you are a debtor—let's say you have a 30-year mortgage loan on a house, or even a 4-year loan on a car—and are repaying your debt in equal installments and inflation causes your income to increase, then you come out ahead. Your debt payments are a smaller percentage of your income than they were when you first took out the loan. In other words, you are repaying the loan with "cheaper dollars." So debtors can come out ahead in periods of high inflation.

Creditors, on the other hand, lose during times of inflation for the opposite reason. Their debt repayments have less value in terms of real purchasing power than they did before. That's why banks and other financial institutions do not like inflation, while people with flexible incomes don't worry about it as much as those on fixed incomes, such as many retired people.

This phenomenon also helps explain why banks and other creditors won't make loans unless they receive interest. The interest helps offset their risk of losing purchasing power to inflation. It also helps explain why many home mortgage loans, credit cards, and other loans now have adjustable rates tied to market interest rates. They help the lender compensate for high rates of inflation and shift the burden to the debtor. There are, of course, other factors involved in determining interest rates, which you will want to consider later.

Any way you look at it, inflation can be a serious problem. It causes uncertainty both for businesses and consumers, and it affects different people in different ways. Inflation erodes the value of people's life savings, and it is, as we pointed out earlier, one of the major concerns of most Americans.

So long as wage increases keep up with the rate of inflation, price increases are, at best, a minor inconvenience. When they don't, everyone faces a major problem. This is why the monetary authorities often worry more about inflation than anything else. And it's why the nagging problem of inflation will be discussed more in later chapters.

Measuring Inflation

When the government announces the change in price levels each month the news usually hits the front pages. The headlines may read: CONSUMER

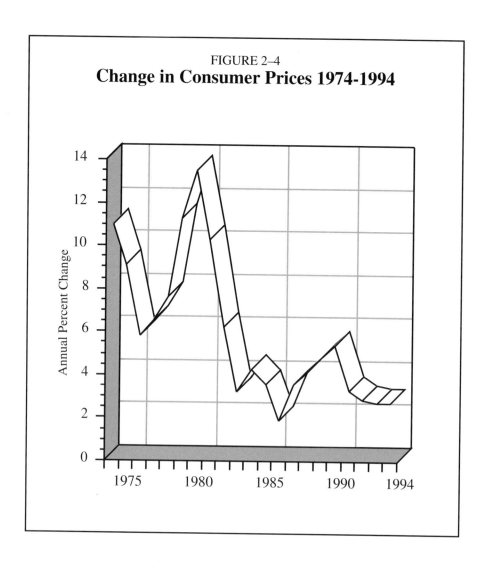

FIGURE 2–4
Change in Consumer Prices 1974-1994

PRICE INDEX UP BY 5 PERCENT, or something similar. That's because inflation affects everyone. Note, also, that they seldom say prices are down because there is almost always some inflation in the economy. Throughout the 1980s, prices increased by an average of 5 percent each year; since then they have been more stable, as shown in Figure 2-4.

Measuring the rate of inflation is a more complex task than it might first appear. There is much more to it than simply keeping track of price changes. Instead, the Bureau of Labor Statistics has constructed an elaborate price index—called the Consumer Price Index, or more commonly the CPI—which measures the changes in the prices of some 60,000 goods and services at different locations around the country. Those prices are then calculated and compared to the price level at some base period, which is set to equal 100 percent. So, if you see that the Consumer Price Index is at 143, that means it now takes $143 to buy what $100 would buy in the base period.

Interestingly, contrary to popular perception, the CPI is not a very good measure of the cost of living. What it does is measure the prices of a fixed "market basket" of products over a given period of time compared to some base year reference point. Seldom, if ever, does an individual's consumption spending pattern coincide exactly with the products selected for inclusion in the index. Nonetheless, like all indices and statistical time series, the Consumer Price Index is a useful tool for economists to gauge the health of the economy. As a rule of thumb, when the CPI is increasing at a rate of more than 5 percent a year, we know something is wrong and the government or the monetary authorities usually act to try to slow the economy down, that is, to slow the rate of inflation. How and why they do that will be examined in later chapters.

> **KEY CONCEPT**
>
> THE CONSUMER PRICE INDEX MEASURES
> THE RATE OF INFLATION BY COMPARING
> THE CURRENT LEVEL OF PRICES FOR A
> SELECTED "MARKET BASKET" OF GOODS
> AND SERVICES TO A SELECTED BASE YEAR.

What Does Inflation Have To Do With Us?

As you have seen, inflation can be your biggest enemy. If your income goes up faster than inflation, then it doesn't matter except that carrying more money can be an inconvenience. If your income doesn't go up faster than inflation, then you are in trouble because your real income—in terms of purchasing power—goes down as inflation goes up. But, more important, inflation can erode the purchasing power of your savings. Suppose, for example, you have $100 in a savings account earning 5 percent interest. At the end of the year you will receive $5 in interest from your bank, giving you $105. But if the rate of inflation is 7 percent, you would need $107 to buy what cost $100 a year earlier, so you lose $2 in purchasing power by having only $105 to show for your investment.

How do you beat inflation? The best way, first of all, is to direct your investments into areas that traditionally provide returns higher than the rate of inflation, And second, remember that time and the power of compounding are on your side. How to put your money into investments that grow faster than the rate of inflation is the topic of a subsequent chapter, so let's focus here on time and the power of compounding. To keep this in context, think about it in terms of your "financial safe." What you're seeing is how important it is to grow the funds inside the safe so they're not eaten up by inflation.

TIME

Remember that *time* is both your ally and your enemy. It's your ally if you recognize the importance of starting an investment and saving program as early as possible. *We can't emphasize that enough,* **UNLESS WE SHOUT AT YOU,** and that wouldn't be polite. The difference between starting to invest $100 a month at age 22 and at age 30 is $68,067.75 by the time you reach retirement age at 65! To put that in perspective, chances are you buy a lottery ticket once in a while if you live in a state that has one. In most lotteries your chances of winning are about 13 million to one, (compared to your chances of getting hit by lightning of 3 million to one). Suppose that instead of buying a lottery ticket, you just invested one dollar a week in a savings account that paid 5 percent interest. If you did that for the average 40 year working life, you would have $6,146.28 at retirement. Not as good as winning the lottery, but a lot more likely to happen, and with about the same effort.

To be more realistic, suppose you set a goal of investing $100 a month by "paying yourself first," and having it taken out of your paycheck and automatically deposited in the bank at 5 percent interest. If you did this for 40 years you would have $151,805 for retirement. What's behind this is the power of compounding, which happens because you earn interest on the interest you have received as it accumulates over time. To make this more clear, look at how much you actually put in the bank over the 40 years you deposited $100 a month. Forty years times 12 months in each year times $100 equals $48,000. But you ended up with $151,805. Why? Because the interest compounded. It didn't take long until you were earning interest on interest as well as your principal. Of course, this only works so long as you leave your money in the bank. The rate of growth of an investment of $100 a month for 40 years is shown in Figure 2-5.

> **KEY CONCEPT**
>
> COMPOUNDING IS WHEN SAVINGS OR
> INVESTMENTS EARN INTEREST ON
> INTEREST AS IT ACCUMULATES OVER TIME.

The Rule of 72

How fast does your money grow? Obviously, it depends on the rate of return, which will vary considerably depending on how much risk you are willing to take. But there's an easy way to find out: simply use THE RULE OF 72, which says that dividing 72 by the annual rate of return will tell you how long it will take for your investment to double. For example, suppose you can find an investment that will pay you 10 percent a year. Divide that into 72 and you will be able to tell how long it takes to double your money at any given rate of interest. That is, 72 divided by 10 equals 7.2 years. At 5 percent return it takes 14.4 years to double your money ($72/5 = 14.4$), which is still not bad, especially when you consider that after your money has doubled once, *it will double again* in another 14.4 years. Such is the power of compounding. Now, perhaps, it is easier to see why we said earlier that we can't emphasize enough the importance of starting early on a regular savings or investment program.

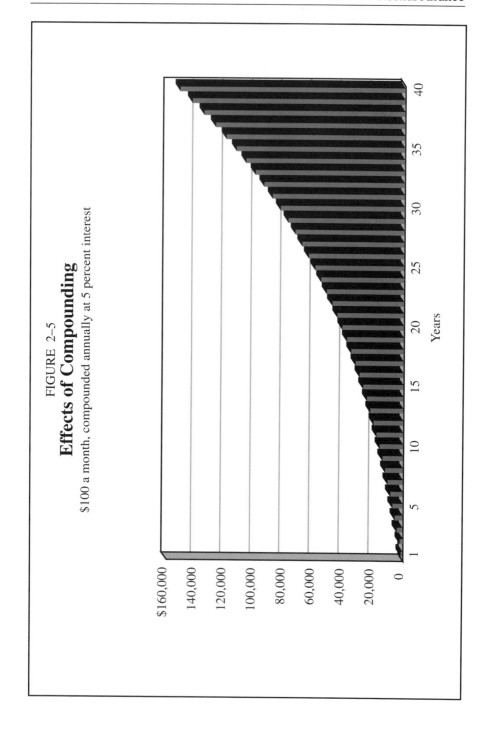

FIGURE 2–5
Effects of Compounding

$100 a month, compounded annually at 5 percent interest

```
-----------------------------------------------------
|                    KEY CONCEPT                      |
|   THE RULE OF 72 TELLS YOU HOW LONG IT              |
|   TAKES FOR YOUR MONEY TO DOUBLE.                   |
|   SIMPLY DIVIDE 72 BY THE ANNUAL RATE OF            |
|                    RETURN.                           |
-----------------------------------------------------
```

TAXES

Finally, there is the question of taxes. Nobody we know likes to pay taxes, but they are, at best, a necessary evil. In any case there has to be some way to pay for the services governments provide, such as roads and bridges, national defense, police and fire protection. So you must pay taxes, and under the system of progressive taxation, the more you make the more you pay. But that doesn't mean you need to pay more than is legally necessary, which most people would agree is probably enough.

Taxes, in fact, are a much more important part of financial planning than is generally recognized. Let's say you have taken all of the advice in this book seriously and are making $100,000 a year. How much tax will you pay? A lot. If you haven't planned for deductions, first there is Federal Income Tax, which can be as high as 39.6 percent of your income. Then there are state income taxes, which can be as high as 12 or 13 percent, depending on where you live. Next you have to consider local or city taxes and probably property taxes, and then whenever you buy anything you will (in most states) pay a sales tax that can be as high as 8 percent. Add all that up and you can easily *pay more than 50 percent of your income in taxes.* So taxes are no minor consideration when it comes to financial planning. Fortunately, there are ways to reduce your tax burden while increasing your wealth at the same time, courtesy of the government.

The Home Mortgage Deduction

The government's biggest gift to taxpayers is the provision in the tax code that allows the interest on home mortgage loans (for both first and second homes as well as anything else that has a bedroom and a bath, like recreational vehicles and yachts) to be deductible for tax purposes. That's no small consideration for most people. In the early years of a mortgage, nearly all of the monthly payments made go to pay interest. Hence, on a $130,000 house the mortgage payments (not counting insurance) may be as much as $1,000 monthly, depending on the size of the down payment. That means a tax deduction of around $12,000 a year, which reduces your tax burden considerably. The advantages of and strategies for buying a house are discussed in more detail in Chapter 3.

Individual Retirement Accounts

Whether you are able to buy a home or not, the next best gift from the government is the Individual Retirement Account, commonly called IRA, which allows qualified individuals to accumulate funds for retirement tax free. Such savings programs compound even faster than the regular contribution programs we examined earlier because contributions to them amount to a tax deduction if the funds are not withdrawn until the individual reaches age 59½. This makes IRAs an extremely valuable way to save for retirement. However, as the current law stands, there are qualifications for eligibility.

```
KEY CONCEPT

INDIVIDUAL RETIREMENT ACCOUNTS ARE
INVESTMENT ACCOUNTS ON WHICH TAXES
ARE DEFERRED UNTIL RETIREMENT.
```

Currently, to be eligible for an IRA deduction there are restrictions on who qualifies and the amount of income earned, especially if you or your spouse participate in another pension plan administered by your employer.[2]

The amounts that can be contributed to an IRA begin reducing when a single person's taxable income exceeds $25,000 annually, and is phased out altogether when income exceeds $35,000. For a married couple filing a joint return, the eligible contributions begin to phase out between $40,000 and $50,000 in annual taxable income. This means, in essence, that IRAs are designed for low and middle class taxpayers. But if you qualify, an IRA can be a considerable tax saving and a huge boost to the rate at which your savings and investments grow. This is shown in Figure 2-6, which compares the rate of growth of $2,000 saved annually with and without the benefits of the IRA tax-deferred deduction. IRAs and other tax-deferred investment opportunities are treated in more detail in later chapters.

---

[2] It is expected that Congress may eliminate these restrictions and make IRAs available to everyone soon.

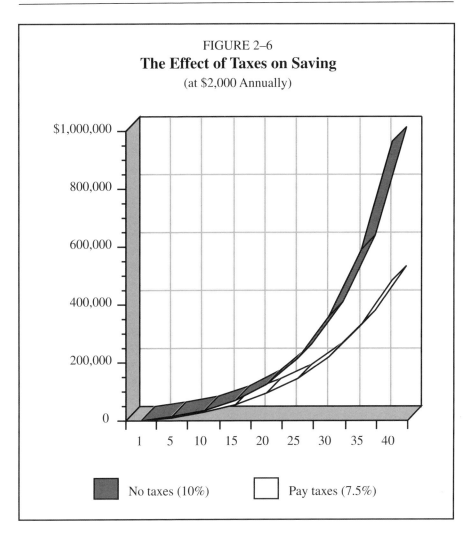

FIGURE 2–6
The Effect of Taxes on Saving
(at $2,000 Annually)

No taxes (10%)   Pay taxes (7.5%)

LOOKING AHEAD

One important point to remember from this chapter is that there are many different ways to save and invest, all of which involve different levels of return and different levels of risk. We have examined the basics of career and financial planning in the context of the things that can help you: education, planning and time, and the things that can hurt you: inflation, taxes and time. Time is the key element either way you look at it. Now we need to take a closer look at the various investment options and opportunities, which are considerable. Then we can look more closely at the specifics of managing your budget and your money—and being sure you hang on to it.

Chapter 3

BUYING A CAR AND A HOUSE, AND INSURING THEM

*I used to think that I was cool, driving
around on fossil fuel, then I found what
I was doin', was driving down
the road to ruin.*

—James Taylor

*In this chapter, we will discuss how to spend money wisely on
major purchases. We're not talking about little things, such as
buying bagels or even paying for vacations; instead, we're
concerned with major purchases that make up a significant
percentage of your annual expenses. We're talking about big
things such as a house, a car, your tax bill and all the different
types of insurance on which you'll spend your hard earned money.
We'll find that how we buy certain items and how much we spend
on them can save us money. We'll also see, yet again, that if we
make time our ally, we can more easily afford these big ticket
items than it might seem at first.*

INTRODUCTION

While the title of this chapter may sound like spending your money,
many of the expenses discussed here are really investments, such as making
payments on a mortgage. This is because a house is the biggest investment

many people will ever have. However, in every case you must shop around to get the best deal before you *spend* your money, so you must apply all you know about being a smart shopper. Remember also that what you'll spend on all the major purchases discussed in this chapter is money you will no longer have for short or even medium term goals. So you must learn to be selective.

BUYING A CAR

To many people, a car is not merely transportation. It's a reflection of tastes, wealth, and identity. A car may also your first major purchase in life. Those things combined lead to many mistakes for first-time car buyers. But, for a moment, set aside these emotional aspects of buying a car and consider your car simply as an investment, though not a very good one— unless of course you have a mint condition classic Corvette with 5 miles on the odometer just sitting in a garage somewhere.

From a strictly financial point of view, a car is considered a **depreciating asset**. That means it's worth less as time goes on. The second you drive it off the dealer's lot, its value starts to fall. Why is that? For several reasons. No matter how often you change the oil, most cars will only last around 100,000 miles; some more, some less. The more you drive it, the more you use up its value. Every year, auto makers change both the styling and technology inside cars, so the further your car lives past the year it rolled off the assembly line, the less stylish and less state-of-the-art it becomes. (The only common consumer item that may depreciate faster than a car is a computer.) This quick depreciation has a great impact on using credit to buy a car.

```
KEY CONCEPT
A DEPRECIATING ASSET IS SOMETHING YOU
OWN THAT DECLINES IN VALUE OVER TIME.
```

Let's look at an example to see why. Consider buying a $17,000 car with a $2,000 down payment. For financing, you'll take out a five-year car loan at 10 percent interest. Over the life of that loan, (See Figure 3-1), you are spending about $4,100 in interest. Ouch! That's money you could better use elsewhere. In this case, your monthly payments would be about $320. However, if you saved $7,000 toward the car, you could have about the

	$15,000 at 10% Interest		$10,000 at 10% Interest	
YEAR	BALANCE DUE	TOTAL INTEREST PAID	BALANCE DUE	TOTAL INTEREST PAID
1	$12,565	$1,390	$6,992	$864
2	9,676	2,526	3,670	1,414
3	6,906	3,380	0	1,616
4	3,624	3,922		
5	0	4,122		

FIGURE 3–1
Auto Loan, Two Examples

same payment, pay it off in three years and save yourself about $2,500 in interest charges. So it pays to have a big down payment, and it pays to shorten the life of the loan as much as possible. One way to think about smart car ownership is trying to increase the number of years you'll own the car for free—or without having to make payments on a car loan. In Figure 3-2 you can see what percent of a loan is paid in interest, depending on the interest rate and the life of the loan. What's worse is that some car dealers want to sell you a *used car* for a small down payment and a five-year loan. If a car already has 20,000 or 30,000 miles on it, the car may give out before your car payments stop! In such a case, you're forced to pay off a loan on something rusting in a junk yard.

KEY CONCEPT

DEPRECIATING ASSETS, LIKE CARS, NEED
SPECIAL CONSIDERATION WHEN BOUGHT
ON CREDIT.

When saving for a car, in what type of investments should you put your money? Because most people will own a car for less than 10 years, it makes sense to make your car savings fund a bank account, money market fund or maybe a short-term bond fund (discussed in Chapter 5). And because a car depreciates, as soon as you buy a new one, you should start saving for the next one. By putting away $20 a week in a bank account at 5 percent

FIGURE 3–2
How Interest Rate and Term of Loan Affect Interest Paid

TERM OF LOAN	INTEREST RATE	PRINCIPAL	INTEREST	PERCENT OF LOAN
5 year loan	12	$10,000	$3,346	33%
4 year loan	12	$10,000	$2,640	26%
3 year loan	12	$10,000	$1,957	20%
2 year loan	12	$10,000	$1,297	13%
1 year loan	12	$10,000	$ 661	7%
5 year loan	10	$10,000	$2,748	27%
4 year loan	10	$10,000	$2,174	22%
3 year loan	10	$10,000	$1,616	16%
2 year loan	10	$10,000	$1,074	11%
1 year loan	10	$10,000	$ 550	6%
5 year loan	8	$10,000	$2,165	22%
4 year loan	8	$10,000	$1,718	17%
3 year loan	8	$10,000	$1,281	13%
2 year loan	8	$10,000	$ 854	9%
1 year loan	8	$10,000	$ 438	4%

interest, after six years you'll have about a $7,300 down payment for your next car.

Also, remember that the car payment is just one cost of owning your car. Gas, maintenance and insurance can easily add more than $2,000 a year to your transportation expenses in your budget. And the bigger, more expensive car you buy, the higher the insurance bill and the more gas it will use. As a rough estimate, you can add $150 to $200 a month above your car payment for these additional expenses, depending on where you live. (See Figure 3-3 for some examples.)

An increasing number of cars are not sold, but leased—which is much like renting a car over a long period. Should you consider leasing? The short answer is no. Leasing usually only makes sense when you must drive a new car for business reasons—or if someone else is paying for it. While the monthly payments may be low, the rules and regulations of a lease are often prohibitive. For example, the lease may say you can drive up to 12,000 miles a year before paying a per-mile charge. If you drive 15,000 miles a year and the per mile charge is 25 cents, you would owe $750 for that year on top of the lease payments. Some leases require you to pay fees when you

FIGURE 3–3
Cost of Operating a Car

	*Ford Escort LX 4-cyl (1.9 liter) 4-door hatchback	*Ford Taurus GL 6-cyl (3 liter) 4-door sedan	*Chevrolet Caprice 8-cyl (4.3 liter) 4-door sedan
Operating Costs	Cents per mile	Cents per mile	Cents per mile
Gas & Oil	4.8	6	6.6
Maintenance	2.4	2.6	2.8
Tires	0.9	1.4	1.4
Total	8.1	10.0	10.8
Ownership Costs			
**Insurance	$875	$716	$749
License, taxes & Registration	$169	$211	$228
Total	$1,044	$927	$987
***Total (per year)	**$2,259**	**$2,427**	**$2,607**

  *   Based on 1995 models
 **   Insurance can vary greatly depending on area and age of driver
***   Assumes 15,000 miles driven per year

Source: *Runzheimer International*

turn the car in, or pay high charges up front. And with a lease, you never have the chance to own the car without making payments.

So what's the best way to buy a car? Assuming for the moment that the car's style, horsepower and color aren't important to you, here are some factors to consider:

- Defer buying a car as long as you can so you can save up the biggest down payment possible. Try riding the bus, riding a bike—or walking.

- Consider first the least expensive type of car that's big enough to handle your needs. Two- or three-year-old, low-mileage used cars often make good choices because you don't have to pay the rapid depreciation that occurs in the first two years, the bugs are worked out of it, and you still get a good car, with more gadgets for a lot less.

- When you look at options on the car, remember that frills can really add a great deal to the price. Do you really need power windows and door locks? Special trim? The luxury package? If you can live without them, you may save thousands of dollars.

- Make sure the car has a good record for reliability and safety. Perhaps the best source of this information is the annual *Buying Guide* book published by *Consumer Reports* magazine, available for about $9 in bookstores. Or check your local library. The fewer repairs a car needs, the lower your maintenance costs over the life of the car.

- When you go to negotiate a price for the car, check the price at several dealers. Tell the dealers you're considering buying from someone else, and what their competitors' prices are. Also, you may want to go to the dealer armed with information such as how much it cost the dealer to purchase the car, and rebates available from the car's manufacturer. You can get this data from *Consumer Reports* New Car Price Service. Details are in the Buying Guide.

- Shop around for the best rate on a car loan. The car dealer can offer financing, usually at competitive rates. But rarely is that rate the lowest in town. Some banks give breaks on the interest rate if you have a checking or savings account with them already from which the car payment can be automatically deducted.

- Take good care of your car. Especially remember to change the oil at recommend intervals and have car rust removed before it spreads.

Both these steps will greatly increase the life of your vehicle, and make it more valuable upon resale.

When should you sell your car? First, keep in mind that in any given year, most car repair bills are not even close to the monthly payment for a new car. When you are ready to sell, though, try to sell the car yourself. If you trade it in at a dealership, you'll probably only get the wholesale price. Check with your state's Department of Motor Vehicles to get the details on transferring the car's title and plates. It's not complicated.

INSURANCE ON YOUR POSSESSIONS

Now that you're ready to buy a car, this is a good time to introduce the concept of insurance for your possessions (as opposed to insurance on your life and health, which is discussed in the next chapter). You buy insurance on your possessions for two reasons. First, you want the cash to replace them if they're lost, stolen, or burned. Second, you want to protect yourself from *someone else's loss* resulting from your property. Suppose you run over Mrs. Murphy's cat—by accident, of course—with your car. You need to protect yourself in case Mrs. Murphy sues you for damages. How much can a cat cost? Well, when you add up Mrs. Murphy's pain and suffering, your negligence, not to mention the replacement value of the cat, you could be facing a very substantial judgment. Likewise, if Mrs. Murphy slips and falls on your icy driveway coming to ask if you've seen her cat, she could sue for a lot more. You want to make sure your car insurance and your homeowner's or renter's insurance cover your liability obligations in such situations.

CAR INSURANCE

The time to first think about car insurance is not after you've bought the car, but when you're deciding which model to buy. When you've narrowed down the list, ask your insurance agent for prices. You may find that while you can afford certain cars, you can't afford them *and* the insurance. Here are the typical types of coverage in your policy:

- *Bodily injury liability.* It seems every day we hear about settlements where the injured person receives higher and higher awards for smaller and smaller injuries. To protect yourself from being on the wrong end of one of these lawsuits, make sure your liability insurance covers at least the value of your assets, or more. Many states have minimum liability insurance requirements; your insurance agent can advise you on this.

- *Property damage coverage*. If you run over someone's mailbox or total their car, this part of your insurance will cover the damages.

- *Uninsured or underinsured motorists*. It may sound unfair, but if another motorist doesn't have enough insurance to cover care for your injuries or lost wages, you need to have this coverage. However, if you already have disability insurance, you may not need this. Check it out.

- *Collision*. This covers damage to your car and comes with a deductible. How high should the deductible be? $500? $2,000? If you have money to spare, take a higher deductible and you'll save a lot of money. Of course, the lower the deductible the higher the payments will be, and vice versa. If your car is a real junker, or if its useful life is almost over, you can forego collision insurance because the insurance probably won't cover the replacement cost.

The two sure ways to keep your auto insurance costs low are to have a safe driving record, and to get older! Insurance is based to a large degree on the safety record of other drivers your age. So the older you are, the cheaper your auto insurance premiums. As with any insurance, get quotes from several different agencies before buying.

BUYING A HOUSE

Part of the American Dream is owning your own home. It will most likely be the biggest investment you will ever make. It will probably be the most valuable asset you will ever own as well. In fact, the value of the equity in homes people own in the United States was about $5.6 *trillion* in 1995, more than the value of people's holding in stocks, bonds and mutual funds combined. Why are tens of thousands or even hundreds of thousands of dollars spent on housing? There are many reasons. Here are a few of the most important.

First, with rent, the money you spend every month is gone. Poof. When you leave your apartment, your landlord doesn't hand you a pile of cash and say, "Here's a little something I've been saving up from the rent you've been paying all these years." But as you pay off the *mortgage* (loan) for a house, your *equity* (percent owned) of the house builds. Also, houses in most areas increase in price as time goes by, which is called appreciation.

Unlike a car which you'll recall is a depreciating asset, your house is an **appreciating asset.** All appreciation belongs to the homeowner. So the house becomes an asset that increases in value over time. When you sell your home and move to a new house, you can keep the profit or reinvest it in a more expensive home, which increases your assets. There are cases where real estate values have declined in depressed areas, but they're fairly rare.

KEY CONCEPT

AN APPRECIATING ASSET, LIKE A HOUSE, IS
SOMETHING YOU OWN THAT (USUALLY)
INCREASES IN VALUE OVER TIME.

Second, while your monthly mortgage payment will probably be more than your rent would have been, it may be comparable to your rent or even less after figuring the tax savings that come with home ownership. To own a home, you have to take out a large mortgage. On such loans you pay interest, and that interest is deducted from your income when figuring your federal income taxes, which reduces your tax bill. In addition, property taxes and school taxes that usually accompany home ownership can also be taken as income tax deductions. As with any loan, part of what you pay is principal, which goes toward repaying the loan, and part of what you pay is interest.

In the case of a 30-year mortgage (the most common kind), the difference is staggering. If you buy a house with a $100,000 mortgage, for example, you not only pay back the $100,000 for the house, you may end up paying *twice that* or more in interest expenses. (See Figure 3-4.) To figure out how much in taxes you'll save by owning a home, multiply your tax rate times the amount of the deduction. If you spend $10,000 a year in (deductible) taxes and interest, and your tax rate is 28 percent, your annual saving is $2,800—a hefty increase in your disposable income that can be invested elsewhere.

Third, the government allows additional tax breaks on owning a home. For example, as long as you move from one house to another and buy an equal or higher priced home, you don't have to pay taxes on your home's increasing value, as you would on other investments you sell, such as stocks.

FIGURE 3–4
How Interest Rate Affects Mortgage Interest Paid

	PRINCIPAL	AMT OF INTEREST
$100,000 Mortgage at 9%	$100,000	$192,000
$100,000 Mortgage at 10%	$100,000	$218,000
Difference:		$ 26,000

FIGURE 3–5
How Loan Amount Affects Mortgage Interest Paid

	DOWN PAYMENT	PRINCIPAL	AMT OF INTEREST
$95,000 Mortgage at 10%	$5,000	$95,000	$205,000
$80,000 Mortgage at 10%	$20,000	$80,000	$173,700
Difference:			$ 31,300

Also, after age 55, you can sell your house and get a (one time only) tax break of up to $125,000 on any gain in your house's value.

Fourth, once you've built up equity in your home, you can apply for what is called a "home equity" loan or second mortgage. The advantage here is that such loans usually carry lower interest rates than credit cards, or other forms of debt, and they provide an additional tax deduction. The disadvantage is that the loan uses your home as collateral, meaning it is used as security pledged against paying the loan off in a timely fashion. So if you can't pay the loan, the lender may seize your home, which is called foreclosure—something you want to avoid at all costs.

Finally, if you like cleaning, fixing and painting things and doing yard work, owning a house is your cup of tea. If you don't like these things, though, you may want to consider renting and invest your money somewhere else. In any case, it's important to remember that buying a house is a big commitment, and its care and maintenance must enter into your quality-of-life calculation.

RENTING VERSUS BUYING A HOME

Now let's take a look at renting, which is an option that many choose versus home ownership. By renting, you have hefty expenses both in rent and taxes because you don't get the government's gift of mortgage interest deductions. But when you own a home, taxes are reduced and some of the money you pay is returned to your financial safe in the form of home equity.

CAN YOU AFFORD A HOUSE?

Clearly, there are many benefits of home ownership. Now the question becomes, can you afford to own a house? As with everything in personal finance, this depends on many factors. These include:

- Your monthly income.
- The size of your down payment.
- Interest rates.
- The price of the house.
- How much non-mortgage debt you have.
- How long you intend to own the house.

First, let's consider your monthly income. As a rule of thumb, mortgage lenders don't want the total monthly payment for your house to exceed 30 percent of your gross monthly income before taxes are taken out. So if you make $36,000 a year, then your gross monthly income is $3,000, and the maximum your payment could be is $900 (.30 times $3,000). Keep in mind that your payment includes not just the mortgage, but property taxes and house insurance. Also remember that lenders vary in how much gross income they'll allow for housing costs. Some won't grant 30 percent, some may grant up to 36 percent. It's safe to assume you need an income of about three times your monthly mortgage payment to qualify for a home loan, depending on how large a down payment you make. There are, however, some other considerations.

> **KEY CONCEPT**
>
> TO QUALIFY FOR A HOME MORTGAGE YOU
> WILL PROBABLY NEED AN INCOME OF AT
> LEAST THREE TIMES THE MONTHLY
> PAYMENT.

Getting your financial house in order, as discussed in Chapter 1, is never more important than when you are buying a house. This is because the mortgage lender looks at *all* the debt you'd be carrying if you were granted a mortgage, not just the mortgage alone. For example, most lenders have a limit of 35 or 36 percent of gross income for *all* your credit bills, including your mortgage payment. So if you're locked into a big car loan or have even moderate credit card debt, you may not be able to qualify for the mortgage until they are paid first.

DOWN PAYMENT

By putting more money into a down payment for a house, you obviously reduce the monthly payments. The problem becomes, how much of a down payment do you need? At the heart of this question is The Homeowners Dilemma: if you wait and save for a bigger down payment, you're missing all the tax benefits and equity-building possibilities of owning a home. If you only have a small down payment, you may not be able to buy the house you want. In the event you are able to purchase a home using a small down payment, you will most likely end up with huge mortgage payments that prevent you from achieving other financial goals. If, after you figure in tax savings, your mortgage payment is close to the amount you're paying in rent, it's probably worth it to get into a house as soon as you can. If the mortgage on the type of house you want is considerably higher than the rent you pay, then you may want to wait and save for a bigger down payment.

However, no hard and fast rules apply here. How much difference can a big down payment make? Let's consider two scenarios. First, assume you buy a $100,000 house with a 10 percent mortgage, and you make a $5,000 down payment. Your monthly mortgage payment is $834. Now, suppose you saved and put down $20,000. Your mortgage payment drops to about $700. And over the life of the loan, you save yourself about $33,000 in interest! (See Figure 3-5 for details.) Another factor in down payments is that if you put less than 20 percent of the house value down, your bank or mortgage company may insist that you buy private mortgage insurance, which assures them that they will get their money in case you can't make the payments and have to default on the loan; and that could cost several hundred dollars a year, or more.

If you decide to save for a house, which investments should you choose? Unless you don't plan to buy for many years, you definitely want to keep your home nest egg in very safe investments—those on the first or second tier of the risk pyramid described in Chapter 5. Because owning a home is an investment that cuts taxes, grows in value and can even help toward retirement planning, many people make saving for a house their top priority.

INTEREST RATES

The lower the interest rate for your mortgage, the bigger the house your mortgage lender will let you buy. How can that be? The size of your mortgage payment drops significantly as the interest rate does. For example, let's say you want to take out a $100,000 mortgage that will be paid off in 30 years—a very common situation these days. If interest rates are 10 percent, your monthly mortgage payment will be $877. However, if you can find a 7 percent interest rate, you would pay only $665, a yearly saving of about $2,500. Over the life of the loan, your savings in interest paid on the mortgage would be $75,000! Some methods of reducing that amount even more will be discussed later.

Does this mean you should wait until rates go down? Unfortunately, interest rates are among the hardest of all economic statistics to predict. What it does mean is that if you don't own a house yet and rates are relatively low, you may want to consider buying one. Also, if you have a mortgage with a high interest rate, and rates have dropped *at least two percentage points* below your current rate, consider getting a new mortgage, a process called refinancing. The reason to wait for a fall of at least two percentage points is that the costs involved in refinancing don't make it worthwhile otherwise.

HOME PRICE

Obviously, the less expensive the home, the more likely you'll be able to get a mortgage for it. What if you can afford a house, but not the one you want? That leaves you with two options. Either save for a larger down payment so you can someday own a bigger home, or go ahead and buy the smaller home, figuring you'll "trade up" later. Trading up has several advantages. As the price of the smaller home appreciates, you're building value in that house you can someday apply toward the bigger home. And the tax benefits of owning a home may also help you save more. Finally, by making mortgage payments you're establishing a credit history, which will show lenders in the future that you are responsible enough to handle a loan.

WHICH MORTGAGE TO CHOOSE?

The examples so far have used 30-year, fixed-rate mortgages, though many different types of shorter term mortgages are offered. The basic idea with these mortgages is that in exchange for taking on some risk, or shortening the length of the loan, you may be able to save money. A common alternative is the 15-year mortgage—half the time, but not double the payments because you're substantially reducing the amount of interest paid. Just as interest compounding works to build your wealth (as discussed in Chapter 2), it also serves to multiply the interest you pay on a loan. Consider this example: a $100,000 mortgage, 8 percent, 30 years. The interest is $164,000 and the monthly payment is $734. Switch that to a 15 year-mortgage, and the payments go up to $991 a month, but you're only paying $66,500 in interest over the life of the loan. Similar to a 15-year mortgage is a bi-weekly mortgage, where you make half a mortgage payment every other week. Because a year contains 52 weeks, you end up paying the equivalent of 13 mortgage payments a year (26 half payments, or 13 full payments), instead of 12. This cuts the number of years you pay a mortgage to about 23, and the amount of interest you pay to $118,000. The extra money increases the amount of equity in the early years of the mortgage, and saves you interest expense in later years. (See Figure 3-6 for the details of how this all works.)

```
KEY CONCEPT
SHORTER MORTGAGES (OR MAKING MORE
MORTGAGE PAYMENTS) MEAN HIGHER
MONTHLY PAYMENTS, BUT DRASTICALLY
REDUCE THE AMOUNT OF INTEREST YOU
PAY OVER THE LIFE OF YOUR LOAN.
```

Another way of reducing the amount of interest you pay and the life

FIGURE 3–6
Effect of Different Types of Mortgages

	AMOUNT OF INTEREST	PRINCIPAL
$100,000 Mortgage at 8 percent – traditional – 30 years	$164,000	$100,000
$100,000 Mortgage at 8 percent – 15 years	66,500	100,000
$100,0000 Mortgage at 8 percent – biweekly – 23 years	119,000	100,000

of the loan at the same time is to *prepay* your mortgage. Every month when you pay your mortgage, include an additional check that goes directly toward the principal of the house. Let's take the standard 30-year $100,000 mortgage. If you pay an extra $30 a month toward the principal, you'll cut the life of the loan by about five years, and save over $50,000! Your banker should be able to help you set this up.

A different type of mortgage loan that transfers a certain degree of risk onto the borrower—in exchange for the possibility of lower interest rates—is an Adjustable Rate Mortgage (ARM). The interest rate on an ARM is tied to some other widely publicized interest rate, such as the rate for six-month Treasury bills, referred to as the *index* rate. A typical ARM loan rate is the six-month Treasury rate, plus 2 percentage points, called the *margin*. The formula to calculate this is: index rate + margin = interest rate on mortgage. For example, if the Treasury rate is 6 percent, then your interest rate is 8 percent. Sounds simple, but it isn't. ARM loans include all kinds of complicating factors, including:

- *Start rates.* This is a temporary rate you first pay when the mortgage begins, and is typically significantly lower than the rate you'll pay when the formula kicks in. It's best just to ignore the start rate and concentrate on what the mortgage will eventually cost you.

- *Rate caps.* A rate cap is a ceiling built into the loan that is the most a lender can charge, regardless of what the formula says. If you can't afford the maximum, best to rethink the loan.

- *Adjustment periods.* Though the level of the index changes constantly, the rate on your mortgage will change only occasionally, (usually once or twice a year), though some may change monthly.

One of the authors of this book once refinanced his mortgage to take advantage of lower interest rates. At the time, financial experts were urging him to take out an adjustable rate mortgage, which would have started his interest rate at below 6 percent. "Rates won't be going up for a long time," he was assured. "A real bargain," they said. Within a few months of refinancing, rates started to rise and today he'd be paying over 9 percent, instead of the 7 percent he in fact locked into by taking a fixed-rate mortgage. (Figure 3-7 shows how volatile the index rates and interest rates in general can be.) Some studies have shown that over a long term, the right type of adjust-

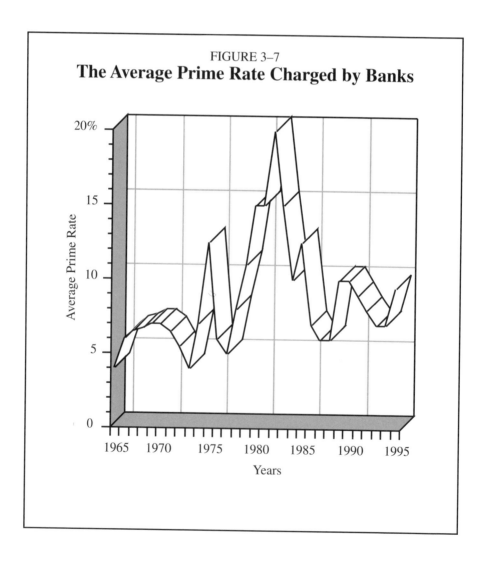

FIGURE 3–7
The Average Prime Rate Charged by Banks

able rate mortgage does save money. However, those periods when the payments in an adjustable rate mortgage run high can upset your financial plan, causing you to forego savings and spending for other things.

INSURANCE ON YOUR HOME OR APARTMENT

One thing you'll also need to consider is homeowner's or renter's insurance. Such insurance covers loss of the dwelling and its contents (not with apartment insurance), from fire, theft or a natural disaster and covers your liability. You can insure your house for a flat amount, or you can insure it for the actual cost of replacing the house—usually a wise idea. A nice feature of such property insurance policies is that for a low cost, you can insure specific items such as jewelry, computers, art, etc. Often it's as simple as sending your insurance agent a receipt showing how much the item cost, or having an appraisal done. As far as the general items inside your dwelling are concerned, your insurance policy will cover them all for a single sum—usually a percentage of the value of your house, in the case of homeowner's insurance. You also can get policies that cover the replacement cost of the items you own, which is probably worth the extra cost. Finally, be sure to take photos or videos of your belongings and keep them in another location other than your house, so you'll have a record in case something happens.

What we've seen so far is that there is a lot more to buying a car or a house than would first meet the eye. But if handled correctly, a lot of money can be saved to put toward building up the contents of your "financial safe" and securing your financial future.

LOOKING AHEAD

Now that we've looked at the basics everyone needs to consider, we must now look at some of the more complicated issues nearly everyone faces. Having children is something most people want to do, and we'll skip the details of how to do it, but once you have children, you have the obligation to care for and educate them—all the way through college. Again, with proper planning, that's not as difficult as it may sound but it's a major consideration in your financial plan. Also, everyone needs to have a life insurance program, which can be partly an investment, but always is a plan to assure that your family is taken care of in case something unexpected happens. Finally, you need to think about retirement and how to have enough money to enjoy it. These are the topics of the next chapter.

Chapter 4

PLANNING FOR KIDS, COLLEGE, LIFE INSURANCE AND RETIREMENT

*Money is like muck, not good
except it be spread.*

—Francis Bacon

*In this chapter, we will discuss some goals that take up a big
portion of your budget. They are very diverse, but all of them can
have a huge impact on your financial future. And in each case,
you are spending money on things that will improve your quality
of life, or the quality of life of someone in your family. Often these
are expenses that, if not properly planned for, have consequences
that can derail a financial plan, or may force sacrifice that proper
planning can avoid.*

INTRODUCTION

Saving your money to buy houses, cars and other big-ticket necessities
is important but that won't buy you a very happy or a very secure financial
future. For many people, those things are important in the pursuit of other
goals, such as raising children, pursuing an education for themselves or for
their kids, or saving for a point in the future when going to work five days
a week can stop, and pursuit of other interests can begin.

HAVING CHILDREN

Obviously, having children is more of an emotional decision than an economic one. But because properly raising a child is one of the biggest expenses in any family's budget, you must consider the costs so that your financial plan is a realistic one. Here is a list of expenses involved in having children, as compiled by the Family Economics Research Group of the U.S. Department of Agriculture:

- *Housing.* Includes a portion of mortgage or rent, maintenance and repairs, insurance, utilities, house furnishings and equipment.

- *Food.* Includes food and drink bought at grocery stores, convenience stores and specialty stores. Also dining out in restaurants and school meals.

- *Transportation.* Includes a portion of the cost of new and used cars, gas and maintenance for the cars, insurance and public transportation.

- *Clothing.* Involves both school and everyday clothing, which wears out fast—but not as fast as kids grow!

- *Health care.* Medical and dental services not covered by insurance, prescription drugs, medical supplies and health insurance premiums not paid by an employer or other organization.

- *Child care and education.* Day care tuition and supplies, babysitting, and elementary and high school tuition, books and supplies.

- *Miscellaneous.* Personal care items, entertainment, reading materials, etc.

The group found that the total cost in raising a child through age 17 (not including college) ranged from $170,920 for the lowest income group to $334,590 for the highest income group (Figure 4-1.) In Figure 4-2 you will see the itemized list of expenses for two income groups. As with any statistic, use these figures with common sense. For example, the house you buy may be big enough for one child, three, or none. And since you'll be paying for heat and taxes no matter how many children live there, those costs don't increase with each additional child. But the numbers give a good estimate on how children will affect your budgeting.

FIGURE 4–1
Cost of Raising Children*

AGE	LOWEST	INCOME GROUP MIDDLE	HIGHEST
<1	$4,960	$6,870	$10,210
1	5,260	7,280	10,820
2	5,570	7,720	11,470
3	6,260	8,600	12,660
4	6,640	9,120	13,420
5	7,040	9,660	14,230
6	7,830	10,580	15,250
7	8,300	11,220	16,160
8	8,800	11,890	17,130
9	8,570	11,790	17,230
10	9,080	12,500	18,270
11	9,620	13,250	19,360
12	11,070	14,870	22,780
13	11,730	15,760	21,490
14	12,430	16,710	24,150
15	15,000	19,890	28,260
16	15,900	21,080	29,950
17	16,860	22,350	31,750
Total	**$170,920**	**$231,140**	**$334,590**

* Based on 1993 dollars

KEY CONCEPT

RAISING CHILDREN PROPERLY CAN BE AN
EXPENSIVE PROPOSITION. MAKE SURE TO
ALLOW FOR IT IN YOUR FINANCIAL
PLANNING.

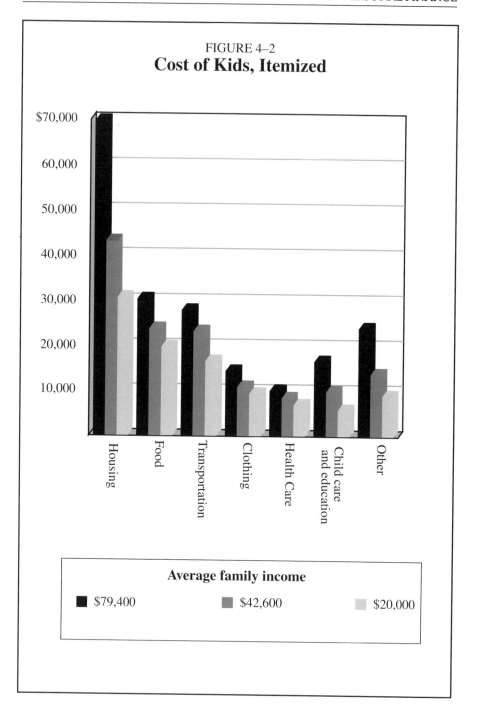

FIGURE 4–2
Cost of Kids, Itemized

PAYING FOR COLLEGE

As discussed in Chapter 2, a college education is one of the best ways to increase your income by preparing you for a job with more opportunity for satisfaction and advancement. The problem, of course, is paying for it. In recent years college costs have risen at twice the rate of inflation, making college financing an even bigger problem for most Americans than it once was. (See Figure 4-3.) The two main ways of paying for a college education are through financial aid and through savings—or a combination of both. If you will attend college soon, expect that a four-year degree (including tuition, room, board and books) will cost roughly $30,000 for a state school, and about $80,000 for a private school. If you're saving for a three-year-old, consider that some estimates put a state education at $72,000 and a private education at $192,000 in the year 2010. Needless to say, those are big numbers.

Unless you are awarded a full scholarship, you may have to pay for your education by:

- Saving and investing before college.
- Borrowing against parents' existing assets to pay school bills.
- Loan programs for students.

A college education usually means higher income even after deducting college loans from a graduate's salary. However, saving for college costs, to avoid borrowing against assets or using loans, has certain advantages. Saving means that graduates won't be burdened with paying off loans early in adulthood when they need to be saving for a new house, car and even socking a little money away for their own retirement. And if parents assume the burden of the loans, it means they must cut back their standard of living and even suspend or curtail saving for their own retirement or other financial goals. Saving can also mean the difference between attending a school of choice, or being forced to attend the school that's most affordable.

There are, however, a couple of catches. Saving for a child's college education has some tax advantages, but not nearly so many as saving in tax-sheltered retirement accounts. And most importantly, if you end up applying for college financial aid, *money saved outside retirement accounts may prevent you from qualifying for financial aid.* This tends to complicate things a bit. Read on to find out why.

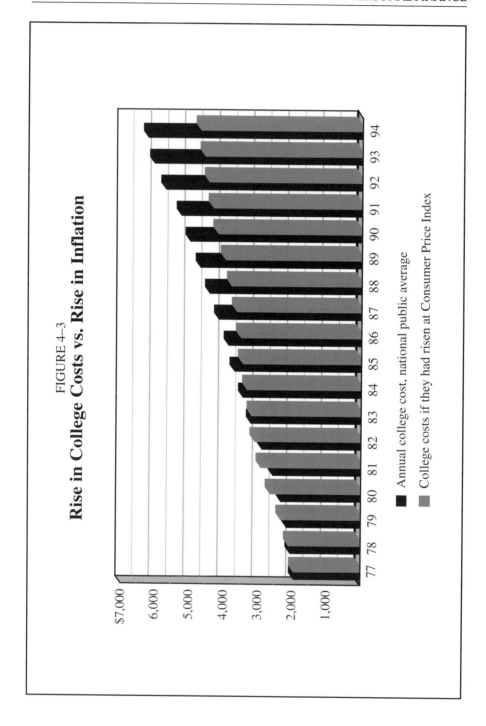

FIGURE 4–3
Rise in College Costs vs. Rise in Inflation

■ Annual college cost, national public average

▨ College costs if they had risen at Consumer Price Index

FINANCIAL AID

Financial aid includes grants and scholarships, loans and work-study programs. Grants, scholarships and loans are available from the state and federal governments, the colleges themselves and many other organizations. Parents seeking financial aid for children usually first fill out the Free Application for Federal Student Aid (check your local high school or college for the form, and be sure to mail it in as soon as you are eligible to do so.) Aid is limited and is awarded on a first-come, first-served basis. By filling out the form, parents essentially divulge their entire financial situation: their assets, liabilities, age, etc. Based on this information, a government agency decides how much you can afford to pay toward college bills, and if you qualify for financial aid. The government does not count money in retirement programs toward your overall wealth, so if you saved money in a retirement tax shelter instead of in a taxable fund for your children, you may be able to get better financial assistance for college. Here are some terms that will help prepare you to apply for financial aid:

- *Expected family contribution*. This is what parents and students are expected to pay toward college based on the Free Application for Federal Student Aid form.

- *Pell Grants*. Money from this program goes to those whose family contributions fall below a certain level.

- *Stafford Loans*. A federal program with loans based on financial need.

- *Perkins Loans*. Based on financial need, Perkins Loans are administered through college financial aid offices. As with Stafford Loans, interest on the loan is deferred while the student is still in school.

- *Parent Loans to Undergraduate Students*. PLUS loans, as they are called, are low cost, and are not based on financial need.

Many financial planning firms specialize in helping parents find their way through the often complex maze of college financing, and can also suggest places to move assets where they won't be counted when applying for aid. The time to first seek their advice is not when your child is in his or her senior year in high school, but when you first start thinking about paying for college expenses. They can also help guide you to organizations such as civic and religious groups, professional organizations, veteran tuition programs or those of unions or employers. Lists of organizations offering this type of help are also available at local and college libraries, and high school guidance offices.

Be sure to inquire at colleges you're considering about work-study programs, which require a certain number of hours worked (generally on-campus) to earn money toward tuition and expenses. However, keep in mind that to get your money's worth out of college, it is a full-time job in itself.

BORROWING AGAINST ASSETS

Presumably once your first child has reached college age, your financial safe has grown in several areas. You own a home, and have contributed money toward your retirement savings plan. These assets can now be used as collateral for low-cost loans. A home equity loan can be a good option here because you can deduct the interest on the loan from your taxes. Borrowing from a retirement savings plan can also provide a low-cost loan. Remember that neither of these lending options is likely to equal the low interest rate in loans through college programs. So make sure you check and see if you qualify for them first. You may also borrow against the cash value of a life insurance policy, and never have to pay the loan back. However, you should carefully compare the benefits of other investments—especially tax-advantaged ones such as a retirement savings plan or a house—before taking out an insurance policy just so you can use it for college costs.

SAVING AND INVESTING FOR COLLEGE

As stated many times earlier, time can be both your ally and your enemy. In no place is this more true than when investing for college. Using the figure of $80,000 for a state university education in the year 2012, if you start today and invest $150 a month with a 10 percent return (after taxes), you'll have more than enough to pay the bills. But if you wait until your child is 10, you're up to about $580 a month. Wait until your child is a sophomore in high school and . . . well . . . you'd better count on loans or other borrowing by that time.

The government gives you some help in sheltering money for your child from taxes through the Uniform Gift to Minors Act. The general rules of the Act allow the first $1,200 dollars of income to be tax free. After that point, income is taxed at the *parents'* rate, until the child reaches age 14, at which point the income is taxed at his or her rate, which would be 15 percent. You manage the child's money until he or she turns 18 (some states allow you to keep control until 21, if you stipulate it), at which time the funds are available for whatever purpose they desire—be it the Porsche or college. But keep in mind when applying for financial aid, that 35 percent of a child's assets must be spent for college to qualify for aid, while only about 6 percent of the parent's assets are considered available.

THE BEST WAY TO SAVE FOR COLLEGE EXPENSES

So you've decided to save for college. What is the best investment choice? Because (presumably) your saving will continue over a long time period, you can look to investments that are riskier in the short term, but will give you the biggest bang for your buck over the long term. Growth stock mutual funds typically are recommended for this purpose, and are discussed in more detail in Chapter 5. Next, to add a little less risk to the portfolio, you may consider corporate or government bonds. Zero coupon bonds—when their yield is in the 8 to 10 percent range—may fit the bill. For example, a "zero" costing $240 today will be worth $1,000 in 18 years. Though their value may vary wildly as interest rates rise and fall, you can be sure that the U.S. government will pay them off when they come due; if it doesn't, you won't have to worry about college or anything else. As the first year of college draws near, parents may want to gradually transfer the stock mutual fund investments into something with a stable value, such as money market funds. Most mutual fund companies will be happy to transfer the money in monthly installments. If you're a more aggressive investor, you need not make the transfer at all. Simply cash in mutual fund shares as college bills come due and hope that over the four-year period of college, the return on the mutual fund exceeds that in money markets.

A FINAL NOTE ON PAYING FOR COLLEGE

For most people, college adds up to much more than a classroom education. Often college is the first time young adults live for long periods away from home. It can be a chance to explore and to learn a great deal about many different things. Freshmen enter college expecting to be engineers and graduate as poets, or vice versa. Friends are made that can last a lifetime. And quality of education is an important factor. Students should want to learn from the best in their fields of study, and not go through four years of college with huge classes and no individual instruction.

KEY CONCEPT

MAKE SURE THE QUALITY OF YOUR
COLLEGE EDUCATION MATCHES OR
EXCEEDS THE PRICE YOU PAY FOR IT.

But college also has an economic component to it: how much value does college bring to our financial lives based on what we earn after college, compared to what we spend on college? While you shouldn't let this consideration be the only one that determines which college or university you choose, consider making it part of the decision. For example, many universities will accept credits earned at community colleges toward a diploma. By living at home and attending a community college, you may be able to save thousands or *tens of thousands of dollars* and still finish your education at a large public or private university, if that is your ultimate goal. Or you may find that the average graduates in the major of your choice make as much money attending the state university as they do going to the private college—at less than half the cost. Many families just accept that when their kids graduate from college, they will have as much money getting out as they did going in—none, or worse, be deep in debt with college loans. But if college could be finished with money left over for that first car, house down payment, computer or whatever, imagine how much further along graduates would be on the road to financial health and security.

INSURANCE ON YOUR LIFE

Great. Just when you've allocated money for cars and a house, and insurance for both, there's yet another category to spend money in. Yes, but life insurance is absolutely necessary because you want your loved ones to keep all those things you've bought and that you're saving for in case something unexpected happens. And that's mainly what life insurance is all about: protecting against loss of our income. If you think buying a house or a car is baffling, it's simple compared to life insurance. And besides being complex, most insurance is sold by people who make a commission—often a fat one—from selling you the policy. That conflict of interest is *very* hard to avoid, and means you must be especially vigilant when buying insurance.

INSURANCE ON YOUR LIFE AND HEALTH

Before discussing the different types of insurance in this category, you must first determine how much life insurance you need. This is a very tough question to answer, because it involves so many variables. Since life insurance pays your survivors when you die, the focus of this calculation isn't on you, it's on your survivors and their needs. If you're a young couple with children, your survivors' needs are great. If you have just retired and have a pile of money saved up, your survivors' needs probably are non-existent because your children are grown with jobs, and your spouse has access to your retirement fund. Also, if you have grown children and both you and your spouse work and each make a good wage, your insurance needs are quite different than those of a young family just starting out. To find out how much life insurance you need, try this simple calculation:

A. Take the annual amount of *your* income after taxes (don't include your spouse).

B. Multiply that amount by .8, because family expenses will be less if you're not around to help spend the money.[1]

C. Now multiply the product in B by the number of years your survivors will need to make up your income.

D. Finally, deduct the amount of money your survivors will be receiving from other insurance policies, such as might be offered by your employer.

Here's an example: Ms. Smith is 35 years old and makes $40,000 a year, with two children and a husband at home who doesn't work. After taxes, she pulls in $30,000 a year. That figure multiplied by .8 (Step B) is $24,000. Say that Social Security would pay $20,000 a year in benefits to the family, and the family figures it wants 20 years' worth of life insurance benefits. The difference between Social Security and the estimated annual need is $4,000. That figure multiplied by 20 is $80,000. If Ms. Smith made $80,000 a year, that figure would jump to over $600,000. So one rule of thumb is, the more you make, the more insurance you need so your survivors can live in the style to which they've become accustomed.

---

[1] To be more precise, determine the Social Security death benefit your survivors will be due and subtract from B. Benefits range from about $13,000 a year if you are in your twenties and earn about $20,000 a year with a spouse and a child, to about $24,000 if you're in your forties and earn over $50,000 a year. If your spouse makes more than $20,000, you can pretty much forget the benefits. For an exact amount, contact your local Social Security office.

Again, these are very rough estimates, but you get the idea. Now let's look at the different insurance products and how they stack up.

Term Insurance

This is the simplest and cheapest type of insurance. Usually you pay for coverage year by year. For example, depending on your age you might pay $100 a year or more (called a premium) for $100,000 worth of coverage—if you die, that's how much your survivors would get. At the end of that year, you would have to pay again to receive another year's worth of insurance. You can buy policies that cover you for more than one year. The older you get, the more you pay because the likelihood of your dying increases. Because it is inexpensive, term insurance is particularly good for young families with children whose incomes are small but whose needs are great. Here are a few types of term insurance you'll need to know about:

- *Renewable term insurance.* This means you can get the same policy again the next year without having to get another physical examination (usually required when you first buy the policy). Renewable term is usually better than nonrenewable, because you're guaranteed the option for coverage for years and years; some stop at age 65, but some go on for years more, although usually at declining payout rates. If there's renewable term insurance, of course there's nonrenewable, which is self-explanatory.

- *Convertible or non-convertible insurance.* A convertible policy can be turned into a different type of policy, such as a whole life policy or a universal life policy, which will be explained below. You may wish to keep the convertibility feature if you're going to want life insurance after you retire. A non-convertible policy cannot be converted to a different type of policy.

- *Participating or non-participating insurance.* Participating policies can pay dividends, though with term insurance, they're usually very small. Non-participating policies do not pay dividends.

- *Yearly renewable or level insurance.* Yearly renewable policies are just what they sound like. You renew every year and the price goes up. A level policy means the policy lasts five or ten years, or even longer, at the same price. But at the end of that policy, there's a big jump in premiums.

So how do you know what's a good buy in term policies? Of course, shop around. The insurer will provide you with what your estimated annual payments will be through the life of the policy—that is, should you choose to keep renewing it as far as the policy goes. Simply compare the prices, keeping in mind when you figure that as you get older, your need for insurance will diminish. So when you're 70, if the annual premiums are thousands of dollars, don't be put off. You probably won't need insurance at that point if you've planned properly. Comparing prices becomes complicated when one company offers you a lower price today compared with another policy, but a much higher price at some point in the future. However, through the miracle of mathematics, the insurer can provide you with a single number that reflects the cost of the policy over a specific period. Ask to see that number, called an interest-adjusted net payment index.

Some insurance agents may try to convince you that term policies are poor long-term buys, that you won't be providing for your family adequately. In some cases, that could be true. But keep in mind that the agent is receiving a much bigger commission to sell life insurance products other than term. Don't be dazzled by complex charts you don't understand or made to feel guilty by an agent who implies you're not providing for your loved ones. Stay in control and make a choice based on *your* financial plan and *your* knowledge of your situation.

Whole Life Insurance

With whole life insurance, a portion of the annual premium you pay goes toward the death benefit, but a portion goes into investments, and builds in value over the years. The idea here is that as with any other investment, the value of a whole life policy grows over time. Eventually, you won't have to pay for life insurance at all because the cash value will have grown enough to pay your insurance expenses. Payment for whole life policies usually remains the same each year, however, the payments are much larger than those for term policies. Because part of whole life insurance is an investment, it builds up what is called a *cash value,* which is an amount of money you can claim should you surrender the policy. Aside from cash value, another key aspect of whole life policies is *dividends,* which many pay. If your policy pays dividends, you can apply those dividends toward your next premium, reinvest it with the company, buy more insurance with it, or take it in cash. You can also borrow against the cash value of your whole life policies for whatever reason. So, for example, if you need a low cost loan to help put a child through college, whole life provides an option. If you reach retirement and need extra income, you can essentially borrow

FIGURE 4–4
Comparison of Term vs. Whole Life*

Age	Term Cost	Whole Life Cost	Difference	Difference invested at 8 %
25	$ 119	$ 1,050	$ 931	$ 1,005
26	$ 123	$ 1,050	$ 927	$ 2,087
27	$ 129	$ 1,500	$ 921	$ 3,249
28	$ 135	$ 1,050	$ 915	$ 4,487
29	$ 144	$ 1,050	$ 908	$ 5,835
30	$ 153	$ 1,050	$ 897	$ 7,271
31	$ 164	$ 1,050	$ 886	$ 8,809
32	$ 175	$ 1,050	$ 875	$ 10,495
33	$ 189	$ 1,050	$ 861	$ 12,225
34	$ 305	$ 1,050	$ 845	$ 14,116
35	$ 221	$ 1,050	$ 920	$ 17,141
36	$ 237	$ 1,050	$ 813	$ 18,310
37	$ 254	$ 1,050	$ 796	$ 20,634
38	$ 272	$ 1,050	$ 778	$ 23,125
39	$ 292	$ 1,050	$ 758	$ 25,794
40	$ 316	$ 1,050	$ 734	$ 28,660
41	$ 342	$ 1,050	$ 708	$ 31,707
42	$ 371	$ 1,050	$ 647	$ 38,474
43	$ 403	$ 1,050	$ 748	$ 39,484
44	$ 440	$ 1,050	$ 610	$ 42,211
45	$ 484	$ 1,050	$ 566	$ 46,199
46	$ 532	$ 1,050	$ 518	$ 55,006
47	$ 573	$ 1,050	$ 477	$ 55,006
48	$ 618	$ 1,050	$ 432	$ 59,873
49	$ 688	$ 1,050	$ 362	$ 65,053
50	$ 773	$ 1,050	$ 277	$ 70,557
51	$ 875	$ 1,050	$ 175	$ 76,390
52	$ 1,003	$ 1,050	$ 47	$ 82,662
53	$ 1,138	$ 1,050	-$ 88	$ 82,552
54	$ 1,278	$ 1,050	-$ 228	$ 95,940
55	$ 1,418	$ 1,050	-$ 368	$ 103,218
56	$ 1,548	$ 1,050	-$ 498	$ 110,937
57	$ 1,688	$ 1,050	-$ 638	$ 119,123
58	$ 1,838	$ 1,050	-$ 788	$ 127,802
59	$ 2,008	$ 1,050	-$ 958	$ 136,992
60	$ 2,298	$ 1,050	-$ 1,248	$ 146,603

* based on $100,000 coverage

most of the cash value of your whole life policy, and *never pay it back*. Of course, when you die, the death benefit will be greatly reduced. And, did you know that such life insurance policies are a tax shelter? The primary tax benefit is that while the cash value of your policy grows, it grows tax-free.

Sounds great? Well, consider these two problems with whole life policies: they take a much larger chunk out of your income than term insurance, and the return they pay on your money usually isn't terrific. And if you like keeping track of what your money is doing, whole life policies are frustrating. You can't separate how much of your policy goes to the insurance company, what the interest rate is on your cash value, or how much is going toward the death benefit. To help you think more clearly about this we need to do a comparison between a term policy and a whole life policy. In Figure 4-4 you can see that if you buy term insurance and invest the difference in cost between the term payments and the whole life payments, you'll eventually end up with a cash value that's greater than the whole life policy, eventually. However, keep in mind that the death benefit in the whole life policy and the cash value of the policy will continue to rise beyond the $100,000 mark, while the maximum on the term value will be $100,000.

KEY CONCEPT

WHEN EVALUATING LIFE INSURANCE
POLICIES, CONSIDER THE OPTION OF
BUYING TERM INSURANCE, AND INVESTING
THE AMOUNT SAVED.

For this reason, many investment experts suggest that you buy term insurance, and invest the amount you save from the cheaper rates in a tax sheltered vehicle of your own—such as a 401(k) plan or an IRA, discussed later in this chapter. You may definitely want to consider whole life when you're going to need insurance late in life—because you still have people dependent on you—or if you have a very high income and need additional sheltering from income taxes and estate taxes. Finally, if you're a lousy saver and can't take advantage of other retirement tax shelters, taking out a whole life policy will force you to put money away—a discipline many people find they need.

Universal Life Insurance

Universal life insurance resembles whole life insurance but gives the policy holder more knowledge and decision-making power. With a universal life policy, the premium you pay goes into a fund on which the company pays interest, while also deducting a portion of the fund to pay for term insurance. You can easily monitor how this fund is doing, plus you can skip payments if you like (if you skip too many, you risk losing the insurance, of course). Universal life policies come with a long list of fees, expenses and charges you must consider before buying.

Variable Life Insurance

Variable life insurance can be thought of as mutual funds wrapped in an insurance shell, which is to say it provides tax sheltering and some insurance benefits. You can choose from a variety of mutual funds to invest your money. But when you write a check, it first goes to the insurance company, which takes out a portion for insurance coverage, *and then* takes out some more as a sales charge—around 4 percent. Then the mutual fund company deducts its up-front charges (called load) and fees. *And then* a portion of what you earn from the mutual fund goes to the insurance company. Because your money is subject to all these costs, to get ahead you must be very wise in your selection of mutual funds. Only good growth funds will let your money grow at a decent rate.

As you can see, especially when you get down to variable life insurance, the line between insurance and investments becomes blurred.

DISABILITY INSURANCE

Here's a gruesome thought: suppose you're in an accident, close to death, but just escape the Grim Reaper. Had you died (and had life insurance), presumably your family would be well taken care of. But if you live, your dependents may be worse off financially if you can't go back to work and earn an income. For this reason, you may want to consider disability insurance.

How much do you need? First, check to see if your employer provides this insurance. Then check out what workman's compensation coverage you have (if you're injured in a job-related activity), and what type of long-term disability would be paid to you by the state where you live. Don't count on Social Security payments to help you—few people qualify for disability benefits.

You want to cover most of the gap between what you earn and the income you'd get if you became disabled for a long period. When you figure how much you need, try first to buy disability insurance through your employer or other large association you may belong to—group rates are usually cheaper. The bigger the percentage of your income it will cover, the more it will cost. Also, the longer the insurance will last (one year, five years, until age 65), the more it will cost. It can be very expensive. But remember, all your financial goals can be delayed for years or canceled if you lose your income for even a couple of years.

MEDICAL INSURANCE

While some people consider disability insurance an option, medical (also called health) insurance must be a top priority. You must be able to protect your savings and income from the increasingly high cost of medical care—from a broken arm to major surgery. If your employer doesn't provide it, find some way to afford it. Two key points in medical insurance are the *deductible* and the *co-payment*. The deductible is how much you must pay before your insurance kicks in. So your health insurance may require you to pay the first $100 or $1,000 of a procedure.

The co-payment is like a deductible, but you have to pay a percentage of each medical bill, which can be costly. So if you must pay 25 percent of a procedure up to $1,000, a $50,000 heart bypass would still only cost you $1,000. But you'd pay $500 on a procedure that cost $2,000.

LONG-TERM CARE INSURANCE

First, the good news about medical care when you retire: when you turn 65, you get a government paid-for medical program called Medicare. The bad news is that Medicare only pays for a few months of an extended-care facility (nursing home). If you are in a nursing home for a lengthy stay, most of your assets may go toward paying your bills. Two types of insurance that retirees need to consider, then, are Medigap insurance, which is insurance sold by private companies to pay the deductibles and co-payments of Medicare, and nursing-home insurance, which is also sold by private companies. Nursing home insurance costs several thousand dollars a year—a lot, but remember that care in a nursing home can cost several thousand dollars a *month*.

FIGURE 4–5
Expectation of Life in Years

AGE (YEARS)	WHITE MALE	WHITE FEMALE	BLACK MALE	BLACK FEMALE
0-1	72.3	78.9	64.9	73.4
10	63.2	69.7	56.5	64.9
15	58.3	64.8	51.6	60.0
20	53.6	59.9	47.0	55.1
25	49.0	55.0	42.7	50.4
26	48.1	54.1	41.8	49.4
27	47.2	53.1	41.0	48.5
28	46.3	52.1	40.1	47.5
29	45.3	51.2	39.2	46.6
30	44.4	50.2	38.4	45.7
31	43.5	49.2	37.5	44.7
32	42.6	48.3	36.7	43.8
33	41.6	47.3	35.9	42.9
34	40.7	46.3	35.1	42.0
35	39.8	45.4	34.3	41.1
36	38.9	44.4	33.5	40.2
37	37.9	43.4	32.7	39.3
38	37.0	42.5	31.9	38.4
39	36.1	41.5	31.1	37.5
40	35.2	40.6	30.3	36.6
41	34.3	39.6	29.6	35.7
42	33.4	38.7	28.8	34.8
43	32.5	37.7	28.0	33.9
44	31.6	36.8	27.2	33.1
45	30.7	35.8	26.5	32.2
46	29.8	34.9	25.7	31.4
47	28.9	34.0	25.0	30.5
48	28.0	33.1	24.3	29.7
49	27.2	32.1	23.5	28.8
50	26.3	31.2	22.8	28.0
51	25.5	30.3	22.1	27.2
52	24.6	29.5	21.4	26.3
53	23.8	28.6	20.8	25.5
54	23.0	27.7	20.1	24.8
55	22.2	26.8	19.4	24.0
60	18.4	22.6	16.2	20.3
65	14.9	18.7	13.4	16.9
70	11.8	15.0	10.9	13.8
75	9.1	11.7	8.6	10.9
80	6.8	8.7	6.8	8.4

Source: *U.S. National Center for Health Statistics*

RETIREMENT PLANNING

One of the keystones of a good financial plan is retirement planning. Why is so much time, effort and money spent on something that often seems so far in the future? There are several reasons. First, you may live 20 to 30 percent of your life after you retire. (See Figure 4-5, which shows life expectancy at different ages.) To spend that time without the resources to live comfortably is tragic and unnecessary. Second, the money you save toward retirement can be sheltered from taxes, allowing you to protect your income from taxes and at the same time see your money grow at a faster rate. Finally, that retirement nest egg can be used for things other than retirement, such as emergency funds and a source for college funding. Planning for your retirement involves all the elements of good financial planning discussed so far. You'll need financial discipline, knowledge of investments and the ability to set future goals. And, more than anything, you'll need to be aware of your financial *allies* and *enemies*.

Consider two scenarios. First, the Quicks. They're a couple who never thought much about retirement until they hit age 50, and their last child graduated from college. Retirement was still 15 years away, but they figured, "What the heck, might as well get started early." They put themselves on a budget, tightened their belts and saved $15,000 a year toward retirement by having money deducted from their paychecks and put into a nice, safe bank account at 5 percent interest. When they turned 65, they figured, a nest egg of $324,000 was waiting for them. Not bad, you say? Well . . . consider the effects of our enemies:

- *Inflation*. At 4 percent, that means every dollar saved today will only be worth about 55 cents in 15 years. Though their bank account pays 5 percent, inflation takes back about 80 percent of that. After inflation, that $324,000 has shrunk to about $180,000 in purchasing power relative to when they started.

- *Taxes*. If the Quicks pay 28 percent in taxes every year, that means a 5 percent interest rate is essentially cut down to 3.6 percent. With inflation at 4 percent, the value of their deposit is actually decreasing every year. Taxes and inflation combined have made the anticipated $324,000 shrink to about $145,000.

- *Time*. The Quicks have waited too long to get a real savings plan together. Even if their savings were tax-free, the first $15,000 they

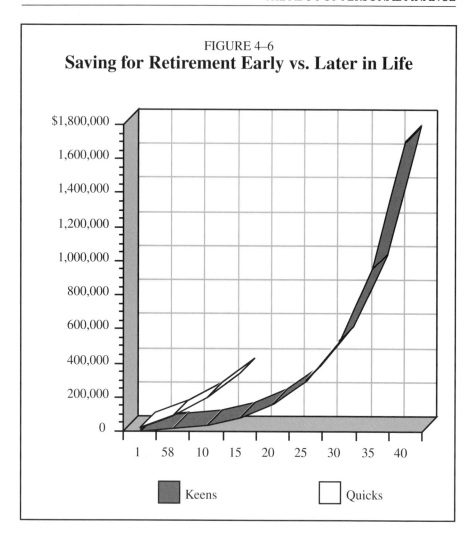

FIGURE 4–6
Saving for Retirement Early vs. Later in Life

invested would only grow to about $22,300 in 15 years after adjusting for inflation.

The bottom line is that though they saved $15,000 a year for 15 years, the Quicks would only have retirement income from savings of about $8,700 a year for the 15 years *after* they turned 65, due to adjustments for inflation and taxes. Better than nothing, but not nearly good enough for secure, enjoyable retirement.

Now let's consider the Keens. The Keens are a couple who both just turned 25. They decide to put away $2,000 a year for the next 40 years in a tax-sheltered investment with a 12 percent return, say, a good stock mutual fund. The Keens are using their financial allies:

- *Education*. They know how certain investments, such as stocks, yield higher returns over time, and they know to put their retirement investments in tax-sheltered accounts. They can also afford to put away $2,000 a year at such an early age because they went to college and have higher than average incomes.

- *Planning*. They have set a future goal and have adjusted their finances to meet that goal.

- *Time*. The value of compound interest here can be used to its fullest extent, because it is given 40 years to work.

When they stop contributing to the retirement account at age 65, they will have about $800,000, which comes out to about $165,000 when adjusted for inflation (over a 40-year period, inflation really hurts). But after post-retirement taxes are paid and the effects of inflation are calculated, the Keens have $28,000 a year to spend until age 80, versus $8,700 for the Quicks. Also, consider that the Keens invested a total of $80,000, while the Quicks invested $225,000.

> **KEY CONCEPT**
>
> DON'T BE QUICK TO PUT OFF RETIREMENT
> SAVING; START WHEN YOU'RE
> YOUNGER—IT'S A KEEN IDEA.

WHERE RETIREMENT MONEY COMES FROM

Your retirement income generally comes from three sources: Social Security, pensions and savings. Social Security is a federally run program that provides income for retired people, benefits for those who have suffered certain misfortunes, and health insurance (Medicare) for retirees. If you're counting on just Social Security to provide for you in your retirement years, you're going to be living a pretty bare bones lifestyle. If you are single and retire at age 65 after earning about $30,000 a year, you'll have less than $10,000 in annual Social Security benefits. And although Social Security payments increase somewhat if you earn more than that during your working life, you won't be receiving much more than that $12,000 a year no matter

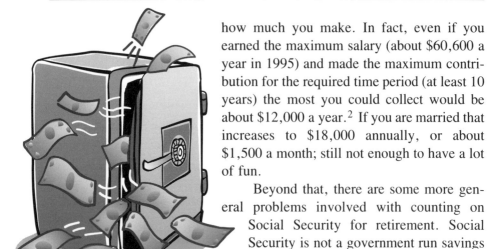

how much you make. In fact, even if you earned the maximum salary (about $60,600 a year in 1995) and made the maximum contribution for the required time period (at least 10 years) the most you could collect would be about $12,000 a year.[2] If you are married that increases to $18,000 annually, or about $1,500 a month; still not enough to have a lot of fun.

Beyond that, there are some more general problems involved with counting on Social Security for retirement. Social Security is not a government run savings program, as some believe. The money deducted from your paycheck in the "FICA" (Federal Insurance Contribution Act) box doesn't end up in a bank account with your name on it where interest is earned until you retire. Instead, Social Security is paid for by people who work now to provide benefits to those who need them now. In other words, the current generation of workers pays for the benefits previous generations are receiving. The problem is that the number of people who will be eligible to draw Social Security benefits in the future is increasing faster than the number of those paying into the system now, so the system is getting squeezed. Can you count on receiving the equivalent of $12,000 a year when you retire? If your retirement is in the next 20 years, probably. After that? You'd better check your crystal ball.

Here are some things you should know about Social Security:

- To be eligible to be fully "insured" in the Social Security system, you must have contributed for 10 years, or 40 quarters (a quarter being a three-month period).

- To receive full benefits, if you were born after 1938, you have to

---

[2]In 1995 the maximum required contribution was 7.65% of wages up to $66,600 or $4,635.90 a year plus your employer's contribution of the same amount for a total of 15.3% or $9,271.80! Any wages you had above $60,600 were not subject to the FICA tax. Note, however, that if your spouse also qualifies for Social Security based on his or her own earnings then both may collect benefits. If not, you qualify for your benefits plus 50% additional for your spouse.

wait until you're *at least* 65 years old to retire. Note also that even though Social Security is deducted from your paycheck automatically, you won't receive payments automatically. Check with your local Social Security office several months before you plan to retire and receive benefits.)

- Because people are living longer, Social Security benefits begin later and later. If you were born in 1960, for example, you'd have to be 67 to receive full benefits.

- If you retire earlier than the age necessary to receive full benefits, you can still get partial benefits. For example, if you can first receive full benefits at 65, you can receive 80 percent at age 62. Some financial experts think this is a good strategy, because you have to live quite a bit longer to make up the difference.

- Increasingly, Social Security benefits can be taxed.

- If you continue working past 65, and don't start collecting, your Social Security payment will increase by about 3 percent a year until you do retire. But if you work and receive Social Security benefits, those benefits are reduced based on how much you're earning. After age 70, however, you can work and earn as much as you can without having your benefits reduced.

- To find out how much Social Security you're due to get, fill out a Request for Earnings and Benefit Estimate Statement, available from your local Social Security office, or by calling 1-800-772-1213.

KEY CONCEPT

SOCIAL SECURITY IS A BIG HELP ON RETIREMENT, BUT DON'T COUNT ON IT TO COVER ALL YOUR EXPENSES.

PENSIONS

Pensions are simply money employers save for you while you work for them—usually some percentage of your income—and then pay to you at retirement. Pensions once were a main source of retirement income, but that is changing. The good thing about pensions is that the money isn't collected from your wages, so no taxes are due until you start collecting. The bad thing is fewer companies offer pensions because of the expense and hassle of managing them. Also, pension payments usually do not increase with inflation after you retire. That means 10 years after retiring, inflation has eaten away about one-third of the purchasing power of your pension dollar, assuming a 4 percent inflation rate. Your employee benefits' office can give you details on pension money owed you.

SAVINGS FOR RETIREMENT

Your savings must make up the difference between what Social Security and your pension will pay for your retirement, and what you need to live comfortably. Fortunately, the tax laws allow quite a few shelters from taxes to help grow your long-term savings. Here is a list of popular retirement tax shelters:

- *IRAs.* Individual retirement accounts may be the greatest thing to happen in a long time for *certain* retirement savers. To see why, let's assume you have some type of retirement plan offered by your employer. If you're single and have an adjusted gross income of less than $25,000 a year, you can put $2,000 into just about any investment under the IRA umbrella and get two tax breaks. The first break is deducting the $2,000 you invest from your taxable income, thus reducing your tax bill. The second break is that the money you put in IRAs accumulates tax free until you withdraw money for retirement after age 59½. You get this same benefit if you're married and your income is under $40,000. Unfortunately, the deduction benefit falls off after that by 10 percent for each $1,000 you earn over the $25,000 single limit and the $40,000 married limit. So if you're married and earn $42,000, your deductible contribution falls to $1,600. You can still put the full $2,000 into an IRA, but you can only deduct $1,600. (Congress is considering liberalizing these limitations.)

If your employer has no type of retirement plan, you can take a full deduction no matter how much you make, but generally, if you take IRA money out before age 59½ you're penalized a lot (the tax on what you withdraw, plus 10 percent.) Other provisos, stipulations and exceptions apply—as with anything having to do with taxes. Should you put money into IRAs even if you don't get the deduction? You must weigh the disadvantage of having your money locked away against the advantage of tax-sheltering. If you're sure you won't need the money and you have at least 10 years to retirement, you're probably better off doing it.

- *401(k).* Next to fully-deductible IRAs, retirement savings plans under section 401(k) in the tax code are tops. Most companies offer these plans. With a 401(k) plan you can have money deducted from your paycheck, which is then put into an account that is tax-sheltered until you retire. The money that is deducted is *pre-tax,* which means the taxed amount on your paycheck excludes the money put into the 401(k). One advantage over IRAs is that the tax deductible amount you can save is larger with 401(k) plans. Currently you can put away about $9,000 a year or 20 percent of your salary, whichever is less. And here's another *big* advantage: many employers match your contributions by 10 percent up to 100 percent. Employers usually offer at least several different types of investments within 401(k) plans, which will be discussed in the next chapter.

- *403(b).* These plans are essentially 401(k)s for employees of not-for-profit organizations.

- *Simplified Employee Pension Plans and Keoghs.* Both these programs are for small businesses or the self-employed. A SEP requires less paperwork than a Keogh, and you don't have to start a SEP the same year you contribute to it, as with a Keogh. However, with a Keogh you can invest more money—up to $30,000 a year versus $22,500 for a SEP.

WHICH INVESTMENTS TO CHOOSE?

Because you're investing for growth and for the long term, the top choice for younger to middle-aged retirement investors is growth-oriented mutual funds. These generally provide the high annual yields needed to put you far ahead of inflation's effects. Mix in a portion of international equity funds for diversification, and possibly some long-term bond funds if you're conservative, and you've created a good retirement portfolio. (See the highlighted blocks on the investment pyramid, Figure 5-2 in Chapter 5.) As you approach retirement, many advisors suggest moving funds down the pyramid to the safest of investments, such as short-term bond funds and bank accounts.

But don't overdo it. Inflation won't stop after you're retired so you still want some growth potential in your pile of investments. How much you keep in stocks depends on several factors, including your life expectancy and the amount of money you have invested. Generally, the larger the amount of retirement investments, the more you can afford to keep in growth vehicles because you won't be needing a lot of it over the short or medium term. So for those without much money it becomes a Catch 22 situation: you can't get more money because you can't invest in growth funds, and you can't invest in growth funds because you don't have enough money. Either way you lose, which is another argument for starting early to build up retirement savings.

Insurance products called annuities offer an alternative for people who don't have access to other tax-sheltered options or who may have a lump sum of money fall into their laps—from an inheritance or selling off an oil well—that they want to invest for a long term. Annuities come in many shapes and sizes, but their basic advantage is that money in them increases tax-deferred (until retirement.) But note that annuities usually have higher costs—much like fees, commissions and penalties for early withdrawals— associated with them than the other alternatives. So before considering an annuity, make sure you're fully funding IRAs and other options. And if you get a lump-sum that's so big you can't put it in an IRA or 401(k) all at once, it may pay to park it in a bank savings account and then deposit it into these other shelters over several years, rather than using an annuity.

Annuities have become much more investor-friendly in recent years by offering more different types of investments, and in some cases, lowering costs. Here is some terminology to give you an overview of annuities:

- Deferred annuities are those used for saving. If you put $10,000 into an annuity today for use when you retire in 40 years, for example, it's a deferred annuity.

- An immediate annuity is one where you start drawing income now for your lifetime. That's right, whether you live to be 100 or just one more year.

- Single premium annuities take one lump sum as their first and only deposit.

- Flexible payment annuities allow you to add to the annuity over time.

- Fixed annuities have a steady return over time.

- Variable annuities allow you to deposit money in mutual funds where your investment will vary in value.

Again, be sure to shop around if you're interested in an annuity. Different firms offer many different cost structures and withdrawal penalties. If the annuity is from an insurance company, be sure to check the health of the company.

GETTING MONEY OUT OF YOUR HOUSE

When you retire, you could sell the house and move into a smaller place, and keep the difference as spending money. The government currently allows you to take up to $125,000 of your profits from a house sale without paying taxes. For some people, the best mortgage of all may be the *reverse mortgage*. Suppose you've paid off the mortgage, retired, and need some extra income. You could sign an agreement with a lending institution that would send you a monthly check in exchange for your house at some point in the future, an agreement called a reverse mortgage. True, you won't have the house to give away in your will, but you'll still be able to live in it while using it as a source of income.

ESTIMATING YOUR RETIREMENT SAVINGS

So, how much will you need in retirement? A good ballpark figure is 80 percent of your current income (this assumes, of course, that you're debt free and paying your bills on time). If you won't have your house paid off until after retirement, add 5 percent to that estimate. If you're an excellent saver and have a high income, cut that to 70 percent. Of course, the farther away from retirement, the harder it is to estimate how much retirement income you need.

The easy way to do these types of calculations is by using special computer programs designed to quickly run through different scenarios. You can adjust levels of inflation, investment returns, and years to retirement in a few seconds. But why not try the old fashioned way. (See Figure 4-8 for details.)

So now you know how much you need to save, which investments are best and what type of retirement vehicles to put those investments in. If the amount to be saved is a daunting figure, now is a good time to review your finances and your priorities. Now IS NOT the time to assume you'll drop dead before you retire or you'll work past retirement age. Just as many people don't like to think about death, many get the same shaky feeling about retirement. Those who set goals for a prosperous and/or early retirement have a better chance of achieving them. Once you have set up your retirement strategy and have confidence in it, don't be obsessed by it. Check back on your investments every so often, and recalculate your saving rate every year or so to make sure you're on track. Recognize that constant tinkering with retirement or any other long-term goal will only drive you crazy,

FIGURE 4–8
Retirement Saving Worksheet
Assumes inflation of 3.5% and investing at 6% above the rate of inflation

A	Retirement income (per year) needed (75 percent of current annual income)	
B	Minus annual Social Security income (deduct $10,000, if you don't know amount)	–
C	Minus any annual pension paid	–
D	Income needed from personal savings	
E	Savings needed to retire at 65 (Multiply line D by 14. This will tell you the total amount saved you will need when you retire)	
F	What you have saved now for retirement	
G	What Line F will be worth when you're 65 (Multiply Line F by appropriate multiplier in attached chart)	
H	What you need to save by retirement (Line E minus Line G)	
I	What you need to save each month to reach retirement goal (Line H x Saving Rate in attached chart)	

Age	Multiplier	Saving Rate
20	3	0.01
25	2.71	0.01
30	2.39	0.02
35	2.11	0.02
40	1.86	0.03
45	1.65	0.04
50	1.45	0.05
55	1.28	0.08
60	1.13	0.15

and may push you to make hasty investment decisions that go against your long-term interests.

LOOKING AHEAD

Now that we've considered just about every type of financial goal and responsibility you're likely to face in a lifetime, it's time to learn about the proper investments to use to save for those goals. Matching investments to goals can be one of the most rewarding aspects of financial planning—some people even find it fun to track their money as it grows and to investigate different types of investments.

Chapter 5

INVESTING YOUR MONEY

Money, it's a kick.
—Pink Floyd

In this chapter, we learn about the different types of investments such as stocks, bonds and mutual funds. Then we learn about matching these investments to financial goals, and ways of balancing investments to get the greatest gain with the least amount of risk. Finally, we learn how we can set up our own portfolio of investments to match our desired degree of risk.

INTRODUCTION

Investments are simply places where you park your money for some period of time hoping to make it grow, and which allow you access to your money when you need it for different purposes. Investments should be thought of as the tools needed to build a large and secure financial safe. In general, investments have two dimensions: how much they pay you, which is called the return, and the degree of risk they have, which of course calls for a chart. As an investor, if you're going to accept investments with more risk, you will want them to pay you a greater return, or else you're not getting a good deal. In Figure 5-1 you see a chart of risk versus return. The lower corner of the chart, Point A, shows how much you can expect to get on your money if you accept no risk. This is represented by bank accounts, for example. Toward the higher end, at Point B, is the stock market, which involves higher risks with the possibility of higher returns. Point D shows investments that carry more risk than they're giving you in return.

This graph is one key to your financial future. The reason is if you

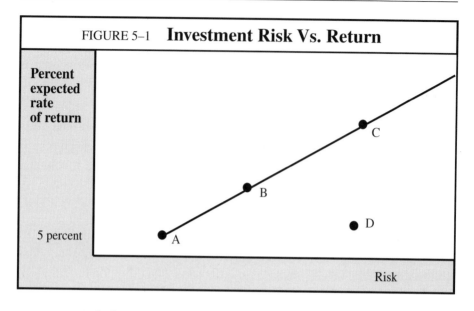

FIGURE 5–1   **Investment Risk Vs. Return**

Percent expected rate of return

5 percent

Risk

want to match the proper investments to your financial goals, you want to travel along that line. If you don't, you're taking too much risk or you're not getting a big enough return. In this chapter you'll look at investments, from the lowest risk to the highest risk, as illustrated in Figure 5-2, the risk pyramid.

The bottom of the risk pyramid lists places to hold your money where you can expect not to lose a penny. The top shows investments where you may lose your shirt. So why would anyone want to put any of their hard earned money at risk? Because by properly taking some risk, you can earn far more money than by playing it safe. And if you remember that time can be an ally when you plan far enough ahead, you can actually reduce the risk to almost zero, while still reaping the extra rewards that riskier investments bring. But remember that staying with the safer, lower yielding investments, has a risk associated with it as well, called inflation.

KEY CONCEPT

RETURNS ON INVESTMENTS VARY
ACCORDING TO THE AMOUNT OF RISK
INVOLVED. THE KEY TO GOOD INVESTING
STRATEGY IS BALANCING RETURNS
AGAINST YOUR TOLERANCE FOR RISK.

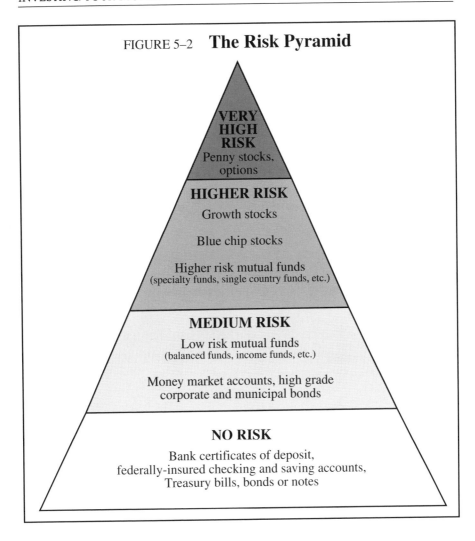

FIGURE 5–2   **The Risk Pyramid**

VERY HIGH RISK
Penny stocks, options

HIGHER RISK
Growth stocks

Blue chip stocks

Higher risk mutual funds
(specialty funds, single country funds, etc.)

MEDIUM RISK
Low risk mutual funds
(balanced funds, income funds, etc.)

Money market accounts, high grade
corporate and municipal bonds

NO RISK
Bank certificates of deposit,
federally-insured checking and saving accounts,
Treasury bills, bonds or notes

CASH AND BANK ACCOUNTS

Almost all commercial banks and savings and loan associations (commonly called "thrifts") carry deposit insurance from the federal government that guarantees deposits up to $100,000. Even when the savings and loan crisis struck in the 1980s and hundreds of thrifts closed, the federal government protected depositors, spending billions of dollars in the process. In a U.S. bank, money is very, very safe. Banks offer a variety of ways to save, including the traditional passbook and statement savings accounts. Banks also offer NOW (Negotiable Order of Withdrawal) accounts, which basically are checking accounts that pay interest. These deposits have historically paid around a 5 percent return.

Certificates of deposit, or CDs, are issued by banks and thrifts and tie up your money for a specific period of time—generally from six months to five years. Cashing in early can require you to pay a small penalty in the form of lost interest. But CDs pay a guaranteed interest rate over a set time span, and come in several forms. You can buy them from your local bank (be sure to check interest rates at other banks to guarantee you're getting the best deal), or you can buy them through a broker who can search the country for the best-paying CD rates. These "brokered CDs" can also be sold on a special market at no penalty, though the price you receive for the CD if you sell it before it matures will change as interest rates vary, just as with bonds.

KEY CONCEPT

THE MOST SECURE WAY TO INVEST YOUR MONEY IS IN BANKS AND THRIFTS THAT ARE INSURED BY THE FEDERAL GOVERNMENT.

MONEY MARKET FUNDS

Money market accounts are investments that operate much like bank accounts. Money market funds are sold by big investment companies. Money market funds invest in short-term, high-grade securities such as Treasury bills, bank certificates of deposit and commercial paper—short-term debt issued by large U.S. corporations in order to earn some interest on extra cash they have. Money market funds have very little risk because of the quality of securities required by regulators and because of the short life of the underlying securities—90 days or less. Some commercial paper may have a life of only a day or two. Money market funds always have a share price of $1, and therefore differ from stock and bond funds, whose share prices rise and fall with the prices of their underlying securities. Many money market accounts offer check writing privileges, which makes them much like bank checking accounts that pay interest. Most banks use the same types of investment vehicles as mutual funds. But bank money market funds tend to pay less than mutual funds, in part because of government restrictions on how bank money market funds are managed.

The type of securities bought for money market funds determines their yields and levels of risk. Those investing in nothing but U.S. Treasury bills —considered the safest investment of all—have no risk so long as the government is around. As fund managers mix in other investments, the risk that some part of the portfolio may default increases. Still, risk remains very low.

BONDS

The most common investments after bank accounts are stocks, bonds and U.S. Treasury securities. Each has its advantages and disadvantages, and in the case of investments, this means each has its own risks and its own rewards. Let's take bonds first and then look closely at stocks and strategies for investing in the stock market.

You can invest money by lending it to big institutions that need to borrow money. The biggest of these is the U.S. government which, through the U.S. Treasury, regularly holds sales of debt securities ranging in maturity from 3 months to 30 years. Similarly, many other countries issue bonds. Towns, cities, counties and states also issue bonds to build schools, roads and other public works projects. Finally, corporations issue bonds for the same reasons they issue stocks—to raise money. Bonds are called "debt" securities because they are loans, putting the issuer in debt to the owner. Because U.S. Treasury securities are backed by the U.S. government, they are considered the ultimate in safe investments. That safety, combined with the huge number of Treasury bonds on the market (equaling $4.8 *trillion* in 1995, which is the total of the U.S. national debt), makes them one of the most popular investments in the world. The longer the term of the security, the more interest the securities will pay. So while a six-month T-bill may pay 5 percent, a 30-year bond may pay 10 percent. The United States government issues three basic types of treasuries:

- *Treasury bills* are securities with maturities of one year or less. The owner does not receive interest payments, but instead buys the bill for less than its face value, the difference being what is called the "discount." The difference between the purchase price and the face value amount, which is paid at maturity, represents the effective interest paid on the bill.

- *Treasury notes* have a term of at least one year, but not more than 10 years. Unlike bills, notes have a stated interest rate and the owner receives interest payments twice a year.

- *Bonds* are essentially the same as notes, but have a maturity term of between 10 and 30 years.

- *Savings bonds* are perhaps the most familiar type of U.S. Treasury security for the small investor. They are sold in values anywhere from $50 to $10,000, and can be bought at banks or from brokers. Owners receive no interest payments, but buy the bonds at a discount of their face value; that means you can buy a savings bond for $25 and collect its $50 face value when it matures in about 10 years.

When you buy a long term corporate or government security, you get interest payments over the life of the bond. When it matures, typically in 10, 20 or 30 years, the holder receives the original price of the bond (its face value) in addition to the interest that has been paid. For example, if you buy a 10-year bond that pays 9 percent for $10,000 (the par value), you receive 9 percent interest payments every year on that par value ($900). At the end of the 10 years, you get the $10,000 back. What determines the price of a bond before it matures is the interest rate it pays compared to what interest rates of other investments are paying at the same time. This is an important question because it makes investing in bonds more risky than it might appear. To see why, look at the following example.

Suppose you buy a $10,000 corporate bond that pays an interest rate of 6.75 percent, or an annual return of $675 ($675/$10,000 = 6.75%). At the time it is issued, similar companies are also paying that rate. But now let's suppose that market interest rates in general rise to 8 percent. Would you still buy the same bond at 6.75 percent? Hardly, because you could get a higher rate somewhere else. Other investors feel the same way, so the value of your bond drops. In fact, your bond drops in value to the point where it yields the same rate of interest as the market is paying on newer bonds. If you wanted to sell your bond now, you'd have to lower the price to $8,000 to make its 6.75 percent yield equal to the market rate of interest of 8 percent (675/$8,000 = 8%).

On the other hand, if interest rates fall lower than the rate your bond is paying, you can come out ahead if you decide to sell it. If the market interest rate falls to 5.5 percent, then anyone who wants to buy your bond would have to pay a premium $12,000 to make it worth your while to sell it. In this case, the premium would make your $10,000 bond worth $12,000 ($675/$12,000 = 5.6%).

KEY CONCEPT

WHEN INTEREST RATES RISE, BOND PRICES
FALL. WHEN INTEREST RATES FALL, BOND
PRICES RISE.

One main difference between various bonds is their risk. Generally, the higher the risk, the more the bond issuer must pay in interest. For example, because every company could get into financial trouble or even go out of business, there is a danger that a corporation's bond could stop making payments to bond holders, or default, on its bonds. Because of the risk inherent in corporate bonds, they pay a higher interest rate than U.S. government bonds so that investors will be compensated for taking the risk that the company could go bankrupt.

If the company is in shaky financial shape, it must pay a much higher interest rate to get investors to buy its bonds. If you buy such a bond—called a "junk bond"—you'll be getting bigger interest payments, but you'll also bear the risk that the company will default on the bond, that is, stop making interest payments. This could be a temporary situation, or might become permanent if the company goes out of business, leaving the bonds worthless. The degree of risk in bonds can be determined from ratings provided by bond companies, the best known of which are Standard & Poor's and Moody's. These companies have developed rating scales that make judging bond safety relatively simple. For example, a "triple A" bond rating means it is the highest quality and safest bond, while a "B" bond belongs to a company in financial trouble that probably won't be able to keep up interest payments. A "D" bond is in default.

STOCKS

Now let's take a look at stocks, which are higher still on the risk pyramid than, say, even triple-A bonds. So why consider stocks? The answer is simple: over time, investing in stocks has increased wealth at a faster rate than other investments, such as bank accounts, U.S. Treasury securities and bonds. There is, however, more risk involved.

By owning a share of a corporation's stock, you are not lending the corporation money. Instead, you literally own a piece of that business. You have a right to a small piece of the corporation's profits, and you own part of its buildings, its land, even its furniture. If the company grows and makes

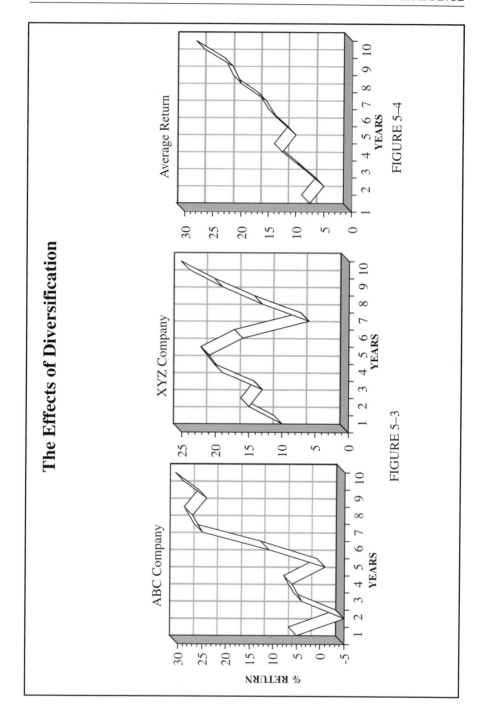

The Effects of Diversification

ABC Company

% RETURN

YEARS

XYZ Company

YEARS

FIGURE 5-3

Average Return

YEARS

FIGURE 5-4

money, your stock grows in price and you may be paid a portion of those profits, called a dividend. While bonds last a limited time, when you buy stock in a company you own a piece of that company for as long as it's in business.

For example, if you had bought $1,000 worth of Walt Disney Company stock (253 shares at $3.95 a share) in 1982, by the end of 1994 those shares would have been worth $11,645. On the other hand, if investors had put $1,000 in Eastern Airlines stock, rather than Disney, in 1982, today they would have nothing, because Eastern went bankrupt in the late 1980s, making its stock worthless. Horror stories such as Eastern Airlines scare many people away from the stock market.

But, on average, stocks do better than any other investment. And as you learned earlier, a higher rate of return—especially over longer periods of time—makes you much more money because of the power of compound interest. That means if you are going to invest in stocks, you need to earn more than you could in more traditional investments while still minimizing your risk. Otherwise it's not worthwhile for you to invest in stocks. The best way to minimize risk with stocks is through *diversification*, which means owning many stocks that operate in different businesses and even in different places—such as Europe or Asia. It also means spreading your investments among stocks, bonds, Treasury securities, and other investment options.

KEY CONCEPT

DIVERSIFICATION MEANS INVESTING IN
DIFFERENT PLACES AND DIFFERENT KINDS
OF INVESTMENTS TO REDUCE RISK.

To understand diversification as it applies to stocks, first look at the simplest case. Assume you take two stocks, ABC Co. and XYZ Co., whose prices have staggered according to the pattern shown in Figure 5-3. As the graphs show, when ABC is up, XYZ is down. But, if you combine the rates of return for both stocks, the end result would be the average rate of return shown in Figure 5-4.

Notice that the graph combining the two has smaller peaks and valleys than if each company is plotted separately. This shows that the average rate of return, and therefore the price of a portfolio containing both ABC Co.

and XYZ Co. will be more stable, and therefore less risky, than ABC or XYZ alone.

Another way to think about this is to consider two companies, let's say one that makes suntan lotion and another that makes umbrellas. When it rains, the umbrella maker prospers; when it's clear, people rush to buy suntan lotion. So Suntan Inc.'s stock rises when Umbrella Inc.'s falls. Owned separately, your investment will have ups and downs according to the whims of mother nature. Owned together, though, the fluctuations tend to cancel each other out.

Fortunately, the answer to getting into the stock market with a minimum of cash and a maximum of diversification is contained in two words: mutual funds. Mutual funds are financial companies where investors' money is pooled. Some mutual fund companies manage as many as 200 stocks; other funds own many more. The fund itself may own hundreds of millions of dollars worth of stocks, but an investor can buy a piece of that fund for as little as $250, or less. A typical mutual fund share might cost about $10 to $30 each, so $250 will buy you 25 shares of a $10 per share fund. A mutual fund share price is simply the fund's worth broken into small units for convenience. The share price is determined by dividing the total worth of investments in the fund by the number of shares in the fund. This figure is called the *net asset value* (NAV). Net asset values are printed in newspaper mutual fund tables, and are a handy way to keep track of how your fund is doing. Mutual fund tables are relatively easy to read and understand.

KEY CONCEPT

THE EASIEST WAY TO DIVERSIFY YOUR
INVESTMENTS IS TO BUY SHARES IN A
MUTUAL FUND.

There are a number of reasons to consider investing in mutual funds. They include:

- *High returns*. The average growth mutual fund yielded a return of about 12 percent for the 10-year period from 1985 through 1994, according to Morningstar Inc., a mutual fund rating agency. This is much higher than returns from many other types of investment, such as bank accounts, certificates of deposit or even U.S. government securities. And as illustrated before, even a couple of percentage points difference in return can make a huge difference in how your money grows over time.

- *Greater diversification at less cost.* If you wanted to buy, say, stocks of 200 different companies on your own, it would cost many thousands of dollars. In fact, some investment experts estimate that to buy enough stocks to get a well-diversified (low risk) portfolio today would cost a minimum of $40,000. But in a mutual fund you can get the same benefits for a few hundred dollars.

- *Professional management.* Full-time financial professionals who use special research and complex investing techniques monitor each stock in the fund, and sell stocks or buy more when they determine the time is right. As an investor you don't have to worry about when to buy or sell stocks.

- *Tremendous ease of investing.* If you want to invest in a portfolio of 200 well-diversified stocks, just send a check for a few hundred dollars to a mutual fund company. When you want to cash it in, just request a check be sent to you.

DIFFERENT TYPES OF MUTUAL FUNDS

Mutual funds come in a variety of different forms, each designed to meet different investors' needs. One fund's objective may be to pay the investor regular dividends; another may pay no dividends but try to increase its share price as quickly as possible. Therefore, prudent investors will want to match their objectives with that of a particular fund. Also you can again use risk and diversification to analyze which mutual funds are best for you. There are several basic types of mutual funds, ranging from equity funds that invest only in stocks to bond funds that invest only in bonds. Which is best for you depends on your tolerance for risk.

Open-end Funds and Closed-end Funds

Funds also can be categorized as either open- or closed-end funds. Most mutual funds are open-end, meaning the number of shares available is always changing, depending on how much money is invested in the fund. The price of the shares is determined by Net Asset Value, as mentioned earlier. Closed-end funds are similar to their open-end cousins in the sense that they can both invest in stocks, bonds, foreign securities, etc. However, closed-end funds raise money just once, and issue a limited number of shares, which are traded on stock exchanges just like regular stocks. Because closed-end funds are priced according to supply and demand—just like stocks—their share price can be above or below the price of the underlying securities.

For example, the price of a closed-end fund might be $16 per share, but its NAV—total value of securities divided by number of shares—is actually $18 per share. Therefore, it is trading at a price of 11 percent lower than its net asset value. Will this fund continue to trade at a discount? Will its share price continue to drop? Nobody knows, because buying closed-end funds requires the type of analysis reserved for buying individual stocks—which means they are not as easy to judge as regular mutual funds.

The demand for different types of funds is reflected in Figure 5-5, which shows that bond and income funds and equity funds are the most popular mutual funds. This is quite a change from ten years earlier, when most mutual fund money was in money market funds. (A list of the different type of funds is seen in the boxed text on pages 102–103.)

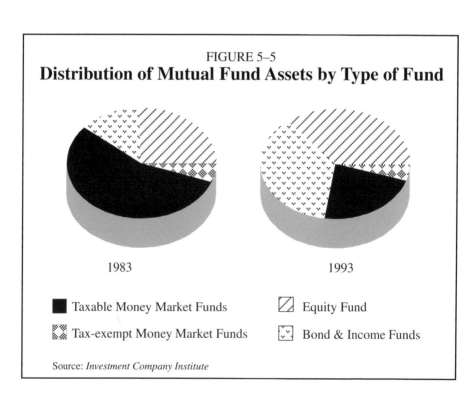

FIGURE 5–5
Distribution of Mutual Fund Assets by Type of Fund

1983

1993

■ Taxable Money Market Funds   ▨ Equity Fund

▨ Tax-exempt Money Market Funds   ⬚ Bond & Income Funds

Source: *Investment Company Institute*

HOW TO EVALUATE MUTUAL FUNDS

With all these different funds to choose from, how do you decide which is best for you? There are three factors to take into consideration: *performance, stability* and *costs.* Performance is determined by how much shares increase or decrease in value over some period of time. Stability refers to dependability of the returns. Do they swing far up one year, then down the next? Costs involve the question of how much the mutual fund company charges for its services.

Performance can be viewed in two ways. A fund's yield is how much income per share it pays to shareholders, made up of both dividends and interest. That income can be reinvested in more shares or paid directly to you. Yield is determined by dividing the income per share by the share price. A fund with a price of $20 per share and income of $2 per share has a yield of 10 percent. Yield is the key statistic when judging bonds, income and money market funds because a fund's total return is its *yield plus the change in the prices of the securities* that make up the fund, whether they are stocks, bonds, or other investments.

A variety of sources exist to find information on mutual fund performance, including magazines such as *Forbes, Money,* and *Consumer Reports.* Also a number of books can be purchased or checked out of your local library. A caution: *be sure to read the fine print in ads for mutual funds* in newspapers and magazines. Some may claim to be the "highest performing," but mutual funds can be categorized in so many different ways that high performance in a small category might not give the whole picture.

The most important rule to remember in judging performance is to look at the performance over a long period of time. Review at least five years, preferably even 10 years or longer. The reason is that any fund manager can have a lucky year or even several years. But how fund managers perform over many years of market swings is the true test of their reliability. Another important rule is consistency of management. If a fund has done well under one manager, and a new manager takes over, should you expect the same performance? Maybe, maybe not. Finally, fund size plays an important part in performance. When a fund gets so big that it can't trade securities quickly or efficiently, fund performance may suffer. Some funds limit their size for that reason.

A fund's **stability** refers to its degree of volatility, which is important to many investors who may have to cash in some of their shares within a year or two. *Forbes* magazine rates mutual fund performance in both rising

Different Types o

Equity Funds

Equity funds, as the name implies, invest only in stocks. But because there are so many different types of companies and investment strategies, this category contains a wide variety of funds. They range from high-risk, growth-oriented funds to relatively stable funds that simply try to perform as well as the market does. Each is described briefly below.

- *Aggressive growth funds* seek to increase stock price, that is, to maximize appreciation as their investment objective. They generally invest in stocks of smaller companies with high growth potential. They often also use risky investment strategies. Growth funds usually show the greatest volatility, but often the highest returns.

- *Global equity funds* invest in stocks all over the world, including the United States. By investing internationally, diversification can be increased in two ways. First, more stocks to choose from means more and different investment opportunities. Second, all countries' economies don't expand and contract in unison. While Germany's economy may be going up, the U.S. economy may be going down, so Germany may provide better investment opportunities at certain times. However, with the benefits of overseas stocks comes an additional risk—that of exchange rates. Overseas stocks must be bought with the currency of the country where that stock is traded. And if the currency of that country rises or falls relative to the U.S. dollar, stocks in that country will become more, or less, expensive to U.S. investors.

- *Growth and income funds* invest mainly in companies whose stock prices are expected to increase at a healthy rate, and which pay dividends.

- *Income-equity funds* invest in companies with good dividend-paying records. Especially key to these funds is the "yield," or the percentage of dividends paid per share price.

- *Index funds* try to match the performance of broad-based stock market averages, such as the Standard & Poor's 500.

- *International funds* invest strictly in non-U.S. companies.

- *Option/Income funds* invest in dividend-paying common stocks on which call options (explained further in Chapter 5) are traded. The objective is high current return.

- *Sector funds* invest only in stocks of certain industries or countries. Because these funds are limited in diversification, they often are more volatile than other funds. Examples are health care funds and biotechnology funds.

- *Socially conscious funds* choose companies according to their records of "ethical" responsibility. These funds may avoid companies that invest in South Africa, or are involved with tobacco and alcohol, nuclear energy or gambling, for example. But the government has no guidelines as to what is "ethical" business, so these funds' investment philosophies can vary a great deal.

Bond Funds

Bond mutual funds invest in federal government, state, and local bonds of varying maturities.

- *Corporate bond funds* usually invest only in corporate bonds. But some also invest in U.S. Treasury bonds, or other bonds issued by federal agencies.

- *Global bond funds* pick debt securities from countries around the world. Again, exchange rate risk is a factor.

Mutual Funds

- *Ginnie Mae funds* (nickname for the Government National Mortgage Association) backs "mortgage securities." When people buy a house, they typically get funding in the form of a mortgage loan. Sometimes these mortgages are sold to Ginnie Mae through the institution that made the loan and then resold to investors. Ginnie Mae guarantees the loan's principal and interest will be paid on time, thus making mortgages more attractive to investors, who will then buy more Ginnie Mae bonds, making more money available for mortgages. Ginnie Mae funds are simply mutual funds that have most of their assets in such securities.

- *High yield bond funds* invest at least two-thirds of their portfolio in lower rated bonds, called junk bonds. A company with a low credit rating isn't in top financial shape, so to sell bonds, it must promise to pay a higher rate of interest to compensate investors for the higher risk of default on the bond. So high yield bond funds pay higher rates of interest, but carry greater risk.

- *Long-term municipal bond funds* invest in bonds issued by governments, including states, cities and towns. Generally governments borrow money through these bonds to build airports, roads, schools, etc. In most cases, income earned by these bonds is exempt from federal taxes. That means interest rates on municipal bonds are usually lower than those paid on corporate bonds because the tax advantages, in effect, boost the money an investor earns. For example, suppose you earned 10 percent on a $10,000 corporate bond investment, or $1,000. But you're in a 30 percent tax bracket, so you have to pay 30 percent of those $1,000 earnings, or $300, in taxes. You really earn only $700. So earning 7 percent on a municipal bond, and paying no taxes, or earning 10 percent on a corporate bond but paying taxes, leaves you with the same final earnings, $700.

- *State municipal bond funds* contain bonds issued in just one state. If you live in that state, income from these bonds is free from both federal and state taxes—depending on your income level.

- *U.S. government income funds* can invest in U.S. Treasury bonds, Ginnie Maes and other government securities.

Mixed Funds

Mixed funds can use a combination of stocks, bonds or money market funds to achieve investment objectives. They include the following possible combinations:

- *Balanced funds* have three goals: To conserve principal (your initial investment), to generate income (through dividends and interest) and to provide long-term growth. To achieve this, balanced funds mix bonds, preferred stocks and common stocks. Preferred stocks get paid dividends before common stocks.

- *Flexible portfolio funds* can be invested 100 percent in stocks or in bonds or in money market instruments, depending on what the fund managers feel is best.

- *Income mixed funds* use both stocks and bonds to achieve a high level of current income for shareholders, through dividends and interest payments.

- *Convertible securities funds* invest in convertible securities, which start out as debt instruments—like preferred stocks—but can be converted into common stock by the investor. If managed properly, these funds can offer both dividend income and the chance to share in a company's growth. However, convertibles are generally not issued by large, strong companies, so they tend to be riskier than other securities.

and falling markets, allowing investors with different risk tolerances to find funds that suit them best. If you're investing over a long period, say because you're young and are saving for retirement, then stability shouldn't matter as much.

Finally, a mutual fund's **costs** are important because costs can reduce the money you earn from investing in the fund. The most important of these costs is the "load," or the money—a sales commission, actually—that you pay to buy or sell shares of a fund. The load is used to pay salespeople such as brokers or financial planners who sell funds. For example, if you invest $1,000 in a fund with a load of 5 percent, $50 is taken from your investment and paid to the salesperson, meaning you actually have invested $950, so your investment has to earn $50 just to break even.

However, a number of low-load (1 or 2 percent) and no-load funds exist. These funds can be bought directly from the mutual fund companies. Interestingly, studies have shown that no great difference in performance exists between load and no-load funds. But if you can buy a fund with no load that has the same performance as a load fund, why pay a load? Loads are capped by law at 8.5 percent.

KEY CONCEPT

MUTUAL FUNDS VARY ACCORDING TO
PERFORMANCE, STABILITY, AND COST.

In addition to loads, mutual funds deduct a certain percent per year from the net asset value of their funds for administrative expenses. The lower this expense the better. Generally 1 percent or less is considered a low expense ratio, while more than 1.5 percent is considered high. One advantage of a large fund is that the mutual fund company can charge a lower percent and still cover its expenses.

KEY CONCEPT

"LOAD" IS THE UP-FRONT FEE THAT IS PAID
TO INVEST IN A MUTUAL FUND.

Another annual cost is the so-called "12b-1" fee, named after the Securities and Exchange Commission regulation that allows them. These fees are controversial because they are often overlooked by investors. They are used by mutual fund companies that don't have their own sales forces, and who can deduct 12b-1 fees to pay for advertising and marketing expenses. Mutual funds can also charge a redemption fee, also called a "back-end" load, meaning you pay a percentage of your fund's value when you sell shares. Often, these fees decrease the longer you own a fund. For example, if you sell your shares after less than a year you may pay a 5 percent redemption fee. Selling in the second year you'd pay 4 percent and so on, until no fee is due after 5 years. Clearly, it is important to make sure you know all the fees and loads you will be paying before buying a particular fund.

WHICH FUNDS ARE BEST FOR YOU?

With more than 5,000 funds to choose from, how do you decide which funds are best for you? It all depends upon your *investment objectives* and your *tolerance for risk*.

Do you want to save money for a big purchase in the future, such as sending your 3-year-old to college or building a nest egg for retirement? Then growth funds may be your best bet. Growth funds during the 10 years before 1994 yielded more than 13 percent, on average. However, many funds have earned more than 15 percent on average over the same time period. Do you want a better rate than you're getting on the savings account at your bank? Then money market funds may be the ticket. Do you need a high amount of current income? Bond funds could be the way to go. Figure 5-6 shows the relative performance of the different types of funds for the 10-year period through 1994.

Most investors have a number of different goals, so they often buy several types of mutual funds. For example, if you're investing for growth, why not invest in two or three funds, thereby giving yourself even more diversification. Should your portfolio have overseas stocks for diversification? Buy an international fund or a global fund.

Once you have determined your goals and found several funds that meet those goals—either by research in magazines, books or from recommendations by your broker or other financial professional—the next step is to get a mutual fund prospectus. A prospectus gives much more detail about a fund than any other source. A prospectus lists how diversified a fund is, its risk factors, investment minimums, fees and expenses, investment strategies the managers use and restrictions on how the fund can invest. Once

FIGURE 5–6
Mutual Fund Performance

	1985	1986	1987	1988	1989	1990	1991	1992	1993	1994	AVERAGE PERFORM.
EQUITY											
Aggressive Growth	29.25	12.03	-2.97	15.89	27.45	-8.73	54.51	8.20	18.79	-3.31	13.74
Equity-Income	27.38	17.64	-1.95	17.02	21.39	-6.24	27.20	9.30	13.58	-1.99	11.21
Growth	29.23	15.04	2.90	15.00	28.90	-6.79	36.71	8.45	11.71	-2.06	12.46
Growth & Income	27.41	15.83	2.01	15.08	23.64	-4.61	28.66	8.26	11.09	-1.47	11.45
Small Company	29.84	10.33	-2.57	19.33	23.59	-9.46	50.27	13.71	17.07	-0.04	13.82
World Stock	41.17	33.68	4.88	13.54	21.79	-10.16	20.53	-1.10	31.46	-3.12	13.88
HYBRID											
Asset Allocation	24.74	21.44	8.39	8.14	16.66	-1.09	20.29	6.11	15.44	-3.17	10.63
Balanced	27.68	16.39	1.46	12.34	19.29	-0.47	26.25	6.96	10.82	-2.81	10.72
Convertible Bond	24.54	15.38	-3.96	11.92	14.47	-5.46	27.85	13.78	15.33	-4.11	9.98
Income	22.26	13.21	-0.72	12.77	12.74	0.28	24.06	9.19	13.33	-4.51	9.33
World Bond	25.43	18.03	17.99	4.39	6.14	14.03	13.10	2.01	15.93	-5.77	10.12
TAXABLE BOND											
Corp. Bond	21.61	14.36	2.21	8.69	11.10	6.21	16.43	7.42	10.38	-3.65	8.61
Govt. Bond	18.23	12.14	1.44	6.63	11.93	8.38	14.01	6.10	8.07	-3.55	8.23

Source: *Morningstar Inc.*

you have studied the prospectuses and decided which funds are right for you, simply fill out the application form and send in a check.

INVESTMENT TIMING

Because the stock market is volatile, when is a good time to invest? That's almost impossible to know. Fortunately, a method of investing exists called **dollar cost averaging** that assures you of buying more shares when the price is low than when the price is high. Dollar cost averaging simply means investing a certain amount of money at regular intervals. For example, every month you buy $100 worth of mutual fund XYZ. On the first month, the price is $10 a share, so you buy 10 shares. The second month, the price rises to $15 a share, so you spend $100 and buy 6.7 shares. In two months, you have spent $200 and bought 16.7 shares. Average price: about $12 per share. What if you decided to buy 10 shares a month, instead of investing $100 per month? The first month you would have spent $100 (10 x $10), and the second month you would have spent $150 (10 x $15). Total cost: $250. Price per share: $12.50, or 50 cents more than with dollar cost averaging. Dollar cost averaging guarantees you will buy more shares when prices are lower, so when share prices rise, you'll have more shares on which to make a profit.

KEY CONCEPT

DOLLAR COST AVERAGING MEANS YOU INVEST
THE SAME AMOUNT OF MONEY EACH MONTH,
THUS ACCUMULATING MORE SHARES WHEN
PRICES ARE LOW.

If you don't have the discipline to write regular checks to your mutual fund, some mutual fund companies can help. You can keep a minimum amount in a money market account they maintain, which will be automatically transferred from that account to a stock or bond fund.

BUILDING AND CHANGING YOUR PORTFOLIO

Building your personal portfolio is much like grazing through a long buffet table. You can choose exactly what you want in exactly what proportions. You may leave the line with a plate of meat and potatoes (safe investments), or you may get a side order of something hot and spicy (individual stocks). It all depends on your tastes or your tolerance for risk.

As a matter of strategy, if you are in your 20s and 30s and just starting to invest, you have many years ahead of you to ride out the ups and downs of the market. Therefore, financial experts often advise those just starting out to put a large percent of their investment capital in growth stocks. But, as you enter your 50s, most financial advisors say you should start switching money to less risky investments as you prepare your portfolio for retirement. Finally, as you enter retirement, you want to switch your investments mostly to ones that will guarantee a steady income. Notice though, that some money is kept in stocks to keep some potential for real growth in the portfolio.

SELECTING INDIVIDUAL STOCKS

Now that you've explored the simple ways to invest in stocks and bonds—through mutual funds and following a broker's advice—it's time to take a look at making your own decisions and buying securities for yourself. Knowing how to analyze stocks is a useful skill for many reasons. Buying and selling select stocks can add excitement and some real profits to your portfolio. It can help you understand more about economics and the world around you. Learning more investment language can make you more confident in many ways, from dealing with a broker to understanding the business section of newspapers better. And finally, either directly or indirectly, you will almost certainly own stocks or depend on stocks during your lifetime. Do you have a life insurance policy? Your insurance company invests in stocks. You may have a pension plan where you work. The pension fund invests in stocks. So the stock market affects almost all of us in one way or another. Realizing how stocks and the financial markets affect us also makes learning about securities more interesting.

DIFFERENT TYPES OF STOCKS

A stock can be a sleeper and a dog. It can even be a sleeper and a fallen angel. But it can't be a sleeper and a blue chip. What does this mean? They are labels investors give to stocks. Sometimes these labels are useful, and help you quickly understand the nature of a stock. For example, a dog is a stock in a worthless company. A sleeper is a stock that has greater value than its price would suggest, but hasn't been noticed yet by investors. Let's look at some stock categories to help you analyze stocks better, but first a warning: *All stereotypes are dangerous, and placing a stock in one category doesn't mean it will stay there forever.* In fact, many companies go through cycles during their lives when they may land in several different categories. Today's "high flier" may be tomorrow's "fallen angel." And some stocks could be considered in a couple of different categories at once. But determining which category a stock may fall into will help you decide whether that company is right for your personal portfolio.

- *Blue chip stocks.* A blue chip stock is a stock of a nationally known company that (usually) grows at a steady rate and pays a steady dividend. The name "blue chip" comes from poker, where the most expensive chips are colored blue. Likewise, blue chip stocks are generally priced accordingly, with high prices compared to their earnings. They command high prices because of the steadiness and consistency of their performance. In other words, they are less risky, and investors are willing to pay more for this. Traditionally, blue chip stocks have included such well-known companies as International Business Machines, General Motors, McDonald's and DuPont. The top blue chip stocks are sometimes called the "Nifty Fifty."

However, nothing lasts forever, especially in the stock market. IBM has long led the market in big computers, and became known worldwide as one of the best stock investments. In fact, it was nicknamed "Big Blue," as the bluest of the blue chip stocks. But as personal computers became more powerful, the demand for IBM's big computers fell, causing losses to mount. A radical restructuring of the company followed. Tens of thousands of employees left the company, and IBM's stock price plummeted, increasing again in 1994.

- *Growth stocks.* These are stocks whose earnings are growing at a faster than average rate, with all or most of their profits reinvested in the business. If a company has a return on equity (net income divided by stockholders equity) of 15 percent per year, and doesn't pay any profits out in dividends, it will double its equity value in less than five years. Twice the equity may mean twice the profits and hopefully a doubling of today's stock prices.

Keep in mind, however, that a growth stock is not necessarily a stock of a small company. Some large companies with billions of dollars in sales also plow most of their earnings back into new plants, equipment, and personnel. High annual returns mean they are growth stocks, too.

FUNDAMENTAL ANALYSIS

Now that you understand the different types of stocks that are available, let's look at the several schools of thought in picking stocks. The most common and easy to understand is *fundamental analysis*. Fundamental analysts study the financial statements of a company, look at the company management, its business prospects, the industry in which it does business and other related factors to project the likely future performance of the company. Based on that prediction of future performance, a fundamental analyst determines whether the company's stock price is too high (overvalued) or too low (undervalued) in relation to similar stocks. Fundamental analysts buy bargains, or underpriced stocks, hoping that the market will recognize the hidden value in a stock, or hoping that the company will become more profitable, and have its price bid up accordingly.

One of the common tools of fundamental analysts is the **price-earnings ratio** (P/E), the measure of how "expensive" a stock price is related to the company's earnings. No single, useful average for the P/E exists for all companies, because companies can be categorized in so many different ways. However, you can judge something about a company by comparing its P/E to the overall market average—which itself often varies a lot. The market average for P/E often is around 15, meaning the average stock's price is 15 times its annual earnings per share at a certain period in time. The faster a company is expected to grow, the higher its P/E. Often a hot computer or biotechnology firm will trade with a P/E of 25 or even much higher. This means investors are willing to pay a premium for a fast-growing company. Likewise, if a company is in a business with a low growth rate, it may trade at a low price-earnings ratio of 6 or 7.

KEY CONCEPT

A PRICE-EARNINGS RATIO (P/E) IS A
COMPANY'S PRICE PER SHARE DIVIDED BY
ITS EARNINGS PER SHARE.

Now suppose by analyzing a company you determine that its growth rate will either soon increase, or will continue at a high pace, beyond what most analysts think it will. And this stock only trades at a P/E of 13, while companies with the kind of performance you're expecting this one will have are now trading with P/E's of 18. Your stock trades at $26 a share with earnings of $2 a share. (P/E of 13, or $26/$2 = 13). But you feel it should be trading at $36 a share (P/E of 18, or $36/$2). You'd buy this stock, and if your reading of the financial tea leaves turns out to be true, you'll see a big gain in your stock. If it isn't, you won't.

TECHNICAL ANALYSIS

While fundamental analysts believe that close scrutiny of financial data and other factors can predict future profits, technical analysis focuses on charts of stock prices and other data, and tries to profit from patterns discerned from charts. If the patterns indicate a future stock price rise, technical analysts buy; if they indicate a drop, they sell. To a true technical analyst (often called a chartist), details such as what the company makes, what its profits are and how its products are selling don't matter. All that matters is the psychology of the market, which they believe can be seen in statistical data like stock price and stock volume movements.

The Dow Theory

Probably the oldest and most respected of all technical theories is the **Dow Theory,** which applies not to individual stocks, but to the whole market. Charles H. Dow, a founder of Dow Jones & Company (publishers of *The Wall Street Journal*, among other things) believed that broad stock market movements predicted economic cycles. These days, followers of the Dow Theory believe that three kinds of price movements exist, with the analogy often drawn to waves in the ocean.

"Primary" moves are seen as tidal changes, when the whole market moves up or down. These trends can last for several years, and foreshadow periods of recession or growth in the overall economy. "Secondary" moves are more like waves, and can occur over a couple months. They can temporarily wipe out the gains or losses of primary moves, but do not halt the overall bull or bear market. Finally, there are ripples, minor price changes, which are seen as meaningless. Dow theorists believe that when the Dow Jones Industrial Average and the Dow Jones Transportation Average both break through their previous peak points, a major new primary move may have started, and that is a ood time to buy stocks.

```
KEY CONCEPT
THE DOW THEORY HOLDS THAT A BIG
MOVE IN THE STOCK MARKET IS SIGNALED
BY THE DOW JONES INDUSTRIAL AVERAGE
AND THE DOW JONES TRANSPORTATION
AVERAGE REACHING NEW PEAKS OR
TROUGHS.
```

The Contrarian School

Another school of technical thought is called the **Contrarian School** of investing, which could best be described as the "learn from the losers" strategy. Basically, contrarians find out what others are doing, because they believe that average investors with only a few dollars invested in the market don't know what they are doing. Measuring what small investors do is easily followed by the odd-lot statistics printed in most newspapers. An odd lot is simply a purchase of fewer than 100 shares of a stock.

Because small investors don't have a lot of money to invest, they generally hold odd lots. So, according to this theory, when small investors are selling stocks, it's time to buy. When they're buying, it's time to sell. Does the odd-lot theory work? During certain periods, small investors have waited until the top of a bull market, bought high and then watched the bear drag down their stock prices However, the reverse has also been true. Odd-lot traders sometimes accumulate shares in periods before bull markets.

Similarly, some contrarians look at mutual funds for their signal of what not to do. When mutual fund managers are leery of the market, and have a relatively large portion of their funds in cash (meaning money market funds) instead of stocks, these contrarians think the time to buy is right.

When mutual fund managers are completely invested in the market, it's time to sell.

```
KEY CONCEPT
CONTRARIANS DO THE OPPOSITE OF
WHATEVER MOST INVESTORS ARE DOING
AT THE TIME.
```

TAKING A RANDOM WALK

What if the fundamentalists and the technicians didn't really know what they were doing? What if the pattern of trading didn't forecast the future? What if all securities were priced just where they were supposed to be, and price changes simply reflected information that popped up randomly and unpredictably, as information is apt to do? Who can predict a technology breakthrough that will strengthen one company and ruin another? Who can predict the death of a key executive? All of these things affect stock prices. In short, what if no way existed to foretell the future and "beat the market" over time? This idea, called the **Random Walk,** holds that if a blindfolded baboon threw darts at the stock pages, it could pick as good a portfolio as a room full of charts and the shrewdest fundamental analyst.

```
KEY CONCEPT
THE RANDOM WALK THEORY HOLDS THAT
STOCK PRICES FOLLOW A RANDOM
PATTERN.
```

Under this notion, except for long-run trends—such as the truisms that the market will increase over time and that stocks of smaller companies will grow faster than stocks of bigger companies—*predicting price changes is impossible because prices follow a random pattern of change*. But, this theory holds water, ironically, only so long as a large number of technicians and fundamental analysts are constantly trying to "beat the market," and therefore bidding the price of stocks up or down according to new information. In other words, the Random Walk theory assumes that information about companies is quickly and efficiently reflected in their stock prices. Therefore, it is also known as the **Efficient Market Hypothesis**.

Different versions of the Efficient Market Hypothesis exist, from that of the true believers, which assumes all information immediately shows up in stock prices, to more specialized versions. Such versions hold that people with inside information, such as company officers and their friends, can beat the market because they have special access to news that will affect a stock's price.

> **KEY CONCEPT**
>
> THE EFFICIENT MARKET HYPOTHESIS POSITS
> THAT SO LONG AS INFORMATION IS
> AVAILABLE TO EVERYONE, THE MARKET IS
> SMARTER THAN ANY INDIVIDUAL IN IT.
> THEREFORE, TRYING TO PICK STOCK
> WINNERS IS FRUITLESS.

The Random Walk is a powerful idea, and many big investors practice it by trying to invest in stocks that mirror the major stock market averages. But to small investors, the Random Walk is comforting because it says that anyone can compete with the professionals if they buy and hold a diversified portfolio of stocks. Put another way, imagine the stock market as the ocean, and the higher the tide, the higher stock prices rise. You are standing on shore at low tide, and you watch as the waves come in and roll out. Will the next wave come in further than the last? No one knows. But over time the tide *will* come in, and you'll be waiting to reap the benefits.

OPTIONS

Stock options give a buyer the right to buy or sell 100 shares of a security at a certain price (called the strike price) before a certain date (the expiration date). Options usually last three, six or nine months. Two basic kinds of options exist: *call options*, which gives the buyer the right to buy securities, and *put options*, which gives the buyer the right to sell the securities. A buyer of calls is hoping that the security's price will rise above the strike price before it expires, so the security can be bought at a cheaper price than the market price, then sold at the higher market price, keeping the difference as a profit (minus the cost of the option).

For example, suppose you expect the price of ABC Corp. to rise above its current $50 per share price, so you buy a call option that has a strike price of $55 per share. The price is $1 per share, or $100 to buy the option because they are bought in blocks of 100 shares. Then, as you expected, ABC rises to $65 per share! You exercise your option, buy 100 shares at $55 each, sell them at $65, and make a tidy $900. (You buy the stocks for $5,500, sell them for $6,500, and deduct $100 for the price of the option.) That profit was earned with only a $100 investment.

The opposite situation occurs when a buyer of puts expects the price of a security to fall below the strike price. When this happens, the buyers purchase the securities at the lower price, then exercise their option to sell them at the higher price.

Few put and call options are actually exercised. Why? Because the prices of puts and calls themselves rise and fall according to the stock prices. If a stock price is $10 above the strike price, and you have a call option that has risen in value to reflect that spread, you simply sell the option to make your profit.

All kinds of strategies exist for using puts and calls, which are generally employed by small investors. At one extreme, puts and calls can be said to limit losses in a portfolio, and so reduce risk. At the other extreme, options can be used to increase risk. For example, an investor can write "naked" puts, which means an option to sell stocks is sold on stocks the option writer *doesn't even own*. If the stock's price rises high enough, the writer could be caught having to buy securities at a high price, and sell them at a low "call" price. So, a good way of looking at options is that they transfer risk. When you buy an option, you are assuming risk, and in exchange, you expect a chance at substantial rewards. Again, options are a form of leverage, borrowing to buy more than you could otherwise, but increasing your risk.

PENNY STOCKS

Penny stocks are stocks of small companies with few or non-existent business operations that generally sell for under $5 per share. Investors are sometimes enticed into buying penny stocks by promises of big returns on small investments. Throughout their history, but especially in the 1970s and 1980s, penny stocks have also been associated with stock fraud and manipulation. In fact, the 1980s saw a proliferation of penny stock brokerage houses—from about 55 in 1984 to about 325 in 1989. Many of these firms were out to make a quick dollar from unwary investors, and this spread of fraud caused the Securities and Exchange Commission to write stiffer rules regarding the conduct of penny stock firms to help protect investors. Buyer beware is the watchword if you want to venture into the penny stock market.

LOOKING AHEAD

What all this adds up to is that in the course of planning for a secure financial future most financial advisors think that employing a variety of investment vehicles is appropriate. As we have seen, there are many ways to do this. The safest and most conservative is investing in bank savings deposits or bank certificates of deposit. Investing in corporate and/or government securities can be a logical addition to your investment portfolio, so long as you remember that there is the risk of losing your capital, especially if interest rates rise. Finally, there is the possibility of putting part of your money in the stock market, where there are hundreds if not thousands of ways to do it. Mostly it all boils down to studying the market or getting some good advice, and then devising a sensible strategy consistent with a tolerance for risk.

Having said that, there is one more thing to consider. Everything we have discussed in this book so far depends on the smooth functioning of the banking system and the overall economy of which it is a part. If the banking system collapses, as is highly unlikely, then we're all in trouble. If the economy collapses, then we are in double trouble. But if they both work the way they are supposed to, as they usually do, then we are all better off.

However, securing our financial future involves more than just personal planning and investing prudently. We also need to understand something about how the banking system works, and how the economy works. And, perhaps more importantly, how we fit into that larger picture. That is the goal of the closing chapter of this book.

Chapter 6

MONEY AND THE BANKING SYSTEM

*There was a cry . . . for more paper
money . . . this currency became by time
and experience . . . never afterward
disputed . . . [but] . . . there are limits
beyond which the quantity may be hurtful.*
—Benjamin Franklin

*In this chapter we will learn about what money is and why it
matters to us in the context of our personal financial planning.
First, we examine the role and uses of money in the economy. We
will find that banks play a much larger role here than we might
have thought. We will look at how banks function and why they
are regulated for our safety, how the amount of money we have
depends on how it is defined, and how money is created by the
banking system. Then we take a look at how banks work, the role
of banks in the economy, and ways to get started dealing with a
bank. Finally, we look at the economy, its condition, and how we
fit into it.*

INTRODUCTION

Before beginning, here's something to think about: in 1995 the total
value of all U.S. coins and currency in circulation was around $390 billion.
Yet according to one definition, the U.S. money supply was just over $1
trillion, or about two and a half times the amount of coins and currency in
circulation. But, according to another definition it was nearly $3.2 trillion,
and according to another it was over $11 trillion. Now, if there are only

$390 billion worth of coins and green paper bills we usually think of as money in existence, how can the money supply be over $11 trillion, some 28 times as much?

WHY MONEY IS MONEY

Money is one of the most mysterious parts of economics and personal finance. About the only thing you can say for sure is that you would all like to have more of it. Money is a source of power and security; and it can certainly make life a lot more enjoyable—but having it doesn't guarantee happiness. Because money is so important, understanding what it is and does merit your detailed attention. You begin with the idea that money has value only if people are willing to accept it in exchange for goods and services. Otherwise, it is just paper and metal disks. It is a piece of paper that has no value whatsoever except to the extent that everyone agrees that it does, and will continue to accept it in exchange for real goods and services.

The Role of Money

To understand the role of money and why it is so important, think what your economic life would be like if you didn't have it. Without money, you would be forced to barter if you wanted to exchange goods or services. That's possible, but it would be very cumbersome and inefficient. Suppose you wanted a new compact disc album. Without money, how would you pay for it? And, just as important, how would you decide what it was worth?

Your only option would be to trade something you own of equal value to the record store for the CD. But what could you trade? Perhaps a case of Coca Cola, or a T-shirt. But where would you get the Coke or the shirt? You would have to trade something for them. Already the process is complicated. At some stage you would have to work and produce something that had value to someone and then go out and find someone who wanted it—and who was willing to trade something you wanted for it, that is, you both would have to have a *double coincidence of wants*, which wouldn't be easy. Clearly, that's not a very efficient way to go about the business of exchanging goods and services. So money, as you will see, makes the process a lot simpler and much more efficient; but money also does more than that.

The Uses of Money

Actually, money has three basic functions. First, it serves as a medium of exchange. Second, it provides a handy measure of value, or unit of account. And, finally, it is used as a store of value.

As a **medium of exchange**, that is, a means of payment, money eliminates the need for barter which, as you have seen, would be very cumbersome and inefficient. Since everyone agrees that money has value and knows that it can always be exchanged for something else, money makes trading simpler. And because money is used, much more trading of goods and services takes place than could happen without it.

KEY CONCEPT

MONEY IS A MEDIUM OF EXCHANGE IN THE SENSE THAT IT IS EXCHANGEABLE FOR ANY GOOD OR SERVICE. THIS MAKES BARTER UNNECESSARY.

As a **measure of value** money eliminates the difficult process of determining what one product is worth in terms of another. Think, for example, of what you can buy with one dollar. Not much, but a dollar will still get you a soft drink, or a couple of candy bars, or perhaps four packs of chewing gum, or a lottery ticket. Because money is the most common measure of value, we are spared the complicated task of figuring out what soft drinks are worth in terms of chewing gum or candy bars or hours of labor because money serves as the common denominator for the value of everything. This attribute of money also simplifies and facilitates the exchange process.

KEY CONCEPT

MONEY IS A MEASURE OF VALUE IN THE SENSE THAT IT ENABLES YOU TO TELL WHAT ONE PRODUCT IS WORTH IN TERMS OF ANOTHER.

Finally, money serves an important role as a **store of value**. As you have seen, people need to be able to save—to buy a car, purchase a house, or live comfortably in retirement. Without money, saving would still be possible, but much more difficult. How could we save without money? One could accumulate stocks, jewels, rare paintings, or other things of value, hoping to be able to trade them for something else in the future. But this would present difficulties.

Suppose you are a farmer with more wheat than you need for your own use. You could store some for a rainy day. But wheat is not readily exchangeable; if you want a new car your auto dealer may not want your wheat because it is bulky to store and must be protected from rain and rodents, and eventually it rots. Clearly, there would be a limit to how long it could be stored. With all these problems in using wheat as your savings account, you decide, instead, to accumulate a herd of cows. But cows have to eat and they take up a lot of space, and eventually they, too, die. So you still have a problem. To store your wealth for the future you need something valuable that is not perishable, something easy to store, and valuable to everyone at the time you decide to use it. Money serves all these purposes.

KEY CONCEPT

MONEY SERVES AS A STORE OF VALUE
BECAUSE IT IS NOT PERISHABLE, IS READILY
EXCHANGEABLE AND PORTABLE, AND IS
EASY TO STORE.

Kinds of Money

In the days before money was a common medium of exchange, many different commodities were used for the purposes just described. Some primitive societies, in fact, used cattle as money. Others used jewelry, such as bracelets or necklaces, and others used precious stones. In the sense that whatever was used as money had an intrinsic value to everyone in society, it served reasonably well as a medium of exchange. Such money is called commodity money, because it has uses in itself as a commodity as well as money. For example, cows have value as providers of milk and beef, as well as possible value as money. Gold is useful for dental work and jewelry, not just as a kind of money.

The most common forms of commodity money, still used today, are gold and, to a lesser extent, silver. Gold was used as money by the Lydians (in what is now Turkey) as early as the 7th century B.C., and it still plays a role in the monetary systems of many nations. Gold meets nearly all of the requirements outlined for money. It is not perishable, and it is easily divisible. Therefore, it can serve as a medium of exchange, as a measure of value, and as a store of value. And, because it has universal value it transcends national boundaries and can be used for international transactions. Indeed, it was used in this way until as recently as 1971.

But gold poses a number of problems as a medium of exchange. To begin with, there is not enough gold to make quantities of it available to everyone. Second, it exists in different levels of purity and quality, which makes it hard to establish a universal value. Third, there is always the temptation to melt it down and re-cast it in a diluted form mixed with something of lesser value, such as silver. And finally, when coined, there is the additional temptation to clip off a tiny piece now and then (which is why many coins have serrated edges.)

Nonetheless, gold has been used as money throughout history, and its use for that purpose gave birth to the modern monetary system. When gold was in its heyday as money in Europe during the Middle Ages and at the beginning of the commercial revolution, it was used almost exclusively as a medium of exchange. Early goldsmiths made their living by coining it and later by storing it for others who didn't want to be burdened by having to carry around all that heavy metal. Gold owners were issued receipts for the gold they had stored with the goldsmiths. And from that came the modern monetary system of banks and of paper money.

People soon realized that rather than exchanging gold when they wanted to purchase something, they could just as easily exchange the receipts, which verified the owner's claim to a given amount of gold stored in some goldsmith's vault. Hence, pieces of paper replaced gold as the medium of exchange.

It wasn't long until some enterprising goldsmith saw a business opportunity, since nearly everyone was exchanging the receipts for the stored gold for money and no one was taking gold out of the vaults. So the goldsmith started acting as a banker, issuing receipts for more gold than he had stored, and in the process collected a fee for storing it. Since the amount of gold actually stored represented only a fraction of the receipts issued for it, the supply of money increased dramatically. From that evolved the modern system of *fractional reserve banking*, which involves much more than gold and paper money. This is barely a hint at this complicated story, but it's an interesting one that has a lot to do with everyone's financial life.

FINANCIAL INTERMEDIARIES

Our banking system functions through about 20,000 financial institutions known as depository **financial intermediaries**. An intermediary is simply a go-between, which serves to bring together savers and borrowers. Commercial banks are the most common and familiar financial intermediaries, but savings and loan associations, savings banks, and credit unions perform many of the same functions. The one thing they all have in common is that they take deposits and make loans. And they all attempt to make a profit on the difference between the interest rate they pay to depositors and the rate they charge on loans. In a very real sense they "intermediate" funds between depositors and borrowers which, as you will see, provides a very important service.

> ### KEY CONCEPT
> FINANCIAL INTERMEDIARIES ARE
> INSTITUTIONS THAT TAKE DEPOSITS FROM
> ONE GROUP OF PEOPLE (SAVERS) AND
> LEND THEM TO OTHER GROUPS
> (BUSINESSES AND INDIVIDUAL
> BORROWERS.)

In addition to their basic role of accepting deposits and making loans, financial intermediaries perform several other basic and important functions. Because they take deposits from large numbers of people and businesses but loan to a much smaller number, they serve a coordinating role, which makes large loans possible. If it were not for financial intermediaries, a business that needed a large loan would have to find hundreds of people willing to lend it money. Clearly this would not be feasible, and if it were, it would be very costly. Financial intermediaries (unlike individuals) can also lessen the risks of lending by spreading loans among hundreds of people and businesses so that if one cannot repay a loan, the loss can be absorbed as a cost of doing business.

Financial institutions also change the time frame for both depositors and borrowers, as they coordinate and make long-term loans from short-term deposits, which is a very convenient service for both groups. Individual depositors usually want to be able to withdraw funds on short notice, whereas many borrowers need long-term loans.

Bank Regulation

Banks and other financial intermediaries operate under a complex web of government regulations. The U.S. banking system functions under two landmark pieces of legislation passed more than 60 years ago. The **Pepper-McFadden Act of 1927** was passed because there was widespread suspicion that the large banks had become too powerful. It effectively prohibited nationally chartered banks from opening branches outside their home states. This reduced their ability to compete with the smaller state-chartered banks and had the effect of keeping all banks relatively small and competitive.

```
┌--------------------------------------------------┐
|                  KEY CONCEPT                     |
|                                                  |
|          THE PEPPER-MCFADDEN ACT OF 1927         |
|                HAD THE EFFECT OF                 |
|          PROHIBITING INTERSTATE BANKING.         |
└--------------------------------------------------┘
```

A few years later the Banking Act of 1933—commonly known as the **Glass-Steagall Act** after its sponsors—put in place even more stringent regulations limiting the power of banks. It prohibited them from selling stocks and bonds, insurance, and real estate. It also set up the first government insurance at banks and thrift institutions. Also, bank deposits and, under the now-infamous Regulation Q, put ceilings on the interest rates banks could pay on savings deposits and prohibited them from paying interest on so-called "demand deposits," which is just another name for checking accounts.

```
+--------------------------------------------------------------+
|                                                              |
|                       KEY CONCEPT                            |
|                                                              |
|             THE GLASS-STEAGALL ACT OF 1933                   |
|             PROHIBITED BANKS FROM SELLING                    |
|         SECURITIES, INSURANCE, AND REAL ESTATE;              |
|           SET CEILINGS ON INTEREST RATES; AND                |
|             ESTABLISHED FEDERAL DEPOSIT                      |
|                       INSURANCE.                             |
|                                                              |
+--------------------------------------------------------------+
```

The legislation of the 1920s and '30s had the effect of ensuring that banks would remain small but profitable. Individuals and businesses had little choice but to deal with local banks and pay whatever interest rates the banks charged on loans while getting low interest payments on their deposits because of Regulation Q ceilings. By the 1970s the rather privileged position banks had enjoyed began to crumble as competing financial institutions entered the market. Among other developments, investment brokers began offering money market funds (deposits secured by very short-term business loans), which paid higher rates of interest than banks were permitted to pay. Also, businesses—especially large corporations—began raising capital through loans to each other. These new practices, and others, put a squeeze on bank profits and spawned new legislation to protect those profits.

Two pieces of legislation in the early 1980s attempted to make the banking system more competitive. One was the Depository Institutions Deregulation and Monetary Control Act of 1980 and the other was the Garn-St. Germain Act of 1982.

These acts phased out the Regulation Q interest rate ceilings on deposits and permitted banks to offer interest on individual checking account deposits (NOW accounts). They also loosened the regulations prohibiting interstate banking and allowed savings and loan associations to offer many of the services commercial banks do with the full protection of federal deposit insurance.

Bank Assets and Liabilities

Banks and other financial intermediaries, like all other businesses, must maintain a balance between their *assets* and their *liabilities*. Assets are what the bank owns; liabilities are what it owes to others, primarily obligations to its depositors. This is most easily understood by examining the combined balance sheet of U.S. commercial banks shown in Figure 6-1.

FIGURE 6–1

The Balance Sheet For All U.S. Commercial Banks

ASSETS (in billions of dollars)	
Securities	$ 946.7
Loans and Leases (Net of reserves for losses)	2,347.7
Interbank Loans	179.8
Cash Assets	218.5
Other Assets	242.7
Total Assets	**3,935.4**
LIABILITIES (in billions of dollars)	
Deposits	$ 2,544.0
Borrowings	639.9
Net Due to Related Foreign Offices	244.5
Other Liabilities	183.3
Total Liabilities	3,611.7
Residuals (assets - minus liabilities)	323.7
Total Liabilities and Equity Captial	**$ 3,935.4**

Source: *Federal Reserve Bulletin*, May 1995

A bank's assets consist of the reserves it keeps at the Federal Reserve Bank—the nation's central bank that serves as the banks' bank—and the cash it keeps in its vaults, the total value of the marketable securities and other investments it owns, the book value of the loans it has made, and other miscellaneous assets.

Its liabilities are the sum of its deposits, some of which are in demand deposits (checking accounts), some in savings accounts, and some in longer-term deposits such as time certificates of deposit, better known as CDs. "Other liabilities" include the amount the bank "owes" to its owners; this amount is the bank's net worth.

The balance sheet for all of the 12,400 banks in the country at the end of 1994 (Figure 6-1) shows that total commercial bank assets were more than $3 trillion. Of those, the 35 largest banks hold more than half the assets. The liabilities of the banks, for reasons you will soon see, make up the U.S. money supply.

THE MONEY SUPPLY

How much money is there? That depends on how you measure it. If you count the currency and coins that you carry around for day-to-day transactions then you don't have very much. At the beginning of this chapter, you were asked to think about why it is that in 1995 the total of all U.S. cash and coins in circulation was about $390 billion. That's a drop in the bucket when you consider that the U.S. Gross National Product for that year (the value of all goods and services sold at the point of final sale) was over $6.5 *trillion*. Cash and coins were only 4 percent of that total. How could such a small amount serve as a medium of exchange for that many transactions? It couldn't even come close. So it doesn't make much sense to limit your view of the money supply to just cash and coins.

Checking Accounts

The vast majority of financial transactions are not made by exchanging cash but rather by writing checks. You probably believe you have money if you have a balance in a **checking account**. To purchase something or pay a bill you write a check instructing your bank to deduct (debit) a certain amount of money from your account and add (credit) it to someone else's. Some 55 billion checks are written in the United States every year. Therefore, to define the money supply more realistically we have to include the total of all funds held in checking accounts. Defined that way, the U.S. had a total money supply of around $1 trillion (including the $390 billion in cash and coins) in 1995.

KEY CONCEPT

A CHECKING ACCOUNT IS AN AGREEMENT WITH A BANK OR OTHER FINANCIAL INSTITUTION TO KEEP FUNDS ON DEPOSIT UNTIL YOU REQUEST THEY BE TRANSFERRED TO SOMEONE ELSE OR RETURNED IN CASH. FUNDS DEPOSITED IN CHECKING ACCOUNTS ARE CALLED DEMAND DEPOSITS BECAUSE THEY ARE AVAILABLE TO DEPOSITORS "ON DEMAND."

Savings Accounts

Most people, however, don't keep much money in checking accounts because—with some exceptions—they don't pay interest. (In fact, money you put into a checking account is an interest-free loan to a bank.) Most of the money in the United States is deposited in **savings accounts**—time deposits—which do pay interest. If you include savings accounts in your definition, then the total U.S. money supply in 1995 was about $4 trillion.

From a depositor's point of view, the only real difference between a checking account and a savings account is that it takes a little more effort to withdraw your money—you have to go to the bank to do it. Liquidity (the ease of converting deposits to cash) is the key factor that differentiates the two types of accounts.

KEY CONCEPT

SAVINGS ACCOUNTS ARE NON-CHECKING
TIME DEPOSITS IN BANKS AND OTHER
FINANCIAL INSTITUTIONS THAT PAY A SET
RATE OF INTEREST.

So if you include savings accounts in the definition of money, (including cash and coins, and checking account deposits), then the U.S. money supply exceeds $4 trillion. That is still less than the value of the Gross National Product and far less than the total amount of financial transactions that take place every year.

Near Money

However, if you extend your measure of the money supply to include any financial instrument that can easily be turned into cash on demand, then you can find a lot more money around. For example, what about U.S. Treasury bonds? Do you own any, or know someone who does? Can they be turned into cash on demand? Of course. So you might want to include government securities in your extended measure definition. The total of all Treasury securities outstanding in 1995 was $4.8 trillion. If you add that $4.8 trillion to the $4 trillion in cash and bank accounts, then the money supply was $8.8 trillion in 1995.

But, if you work at it, you can find more. U.S. dollar-denominated accounts in foreign banks can be converted into cash on demand, so these so-called **"euro-dollars"** can be included in the money supply as well. It's hard to tell exactly how many dollars are deposited in these foreign accounts, but the total is estimated to exceed $2 trillion. Including them in your def-

inition measurement, you can say that the U.S. has a money supply of about
$10 trillion.

KEY CONCEPT

EURO-DOLLARS ARE
DOLLAR-DENOMINATED CHECKING AND
SAVINGS ACCOUNTS IN FOREIGN BANKS.
THESE ACCOUNTS ORIGINATED IN EUROPE,
BUT NOW INCLUDE DOLLAR DEPOSITS IN
ANY FOREIGN COUNTRY.

And then there are many other things you could call money. Deposits
in saving and loan institutions can be turned into cash on demand, as can
deposits in credit unions and mutual savings banks. Also many life insurance
policies have accumulated value that can be turned into cash. Depending on
how you measure it, the U.S. money supply probably exceeds $11 trillion
by the loosest definition, but only $390 billion by the tightest definition—the
total of coins and cash in circulation.

A Formal Definition of Money

Because the government and monetary authorities need to know how
much money is in circulation, more formal definitions have been devised.

The basic money supply is called M1. It consists of the total of cash
and coins in circulation outside of banks plus checking accounts and other
highly liquid financial instruments, such as traveler's checks. A broader,
and more realistic, measure of the money supply is called M2. It includes
everything in M1 plus savings accounts, money market bank deposits and
other short-term, liquid deposits. An even broader measure called M3
includes large, long-term time deposits of over $100,000 and other long-
term deposits. The broadest measure of all, called L, includes some of the
debt instruments that were discussed earlier. All these are summarized in
Figure 6-2.

HOW MONEY IS CREATED

To understand what money really is and where it comes from, you
have to understand what it is that banks do. As you have seen, at the most
basic level banks take deposits and use the money to make loans. The dif-

FIGURE 6–2
U.S. Money Supply 1960-1994

	M1	M2	M3	L
1960	$ 140	$ 321	$ 300	$ 389
1970	214	628	677	816
1980	409	1,629	1,989	2,326
1990	826	3,353	4,126	4,975
1994	1,478	3,600	4,283	5,230

(billions of dollars)

MI = Sum of currency, traveler's checks, and checking deposits
M2 = M1 + savings deposits
M3 = M2 + long term savings deposits
 L = M3 plus other liquid assets

Souce: *Economic Report of the President*, 1994, page 353

ference between the interest they pay on deposits (say, 5 percent) and what they charge on loans (say, 10 percent) is their profit. But there is a lot more going on here than that. In the process, the banking system as a whole creates money—much like the goldsmiths did in earlier times.

This is easier to understand if you trace what happens to a typical bank deposit. Suppose you walk into your bank and deposit $1,000 in cash—payment for two weeks of hard work. Now you have a $1,000 deposit in your checking account. What does the bank do with it? Most surely it is going to lend it to someone else. But, under the system of fractional banking, the bank cannot lend out all of your deposit. It must by law keep a fraction of it on reserve, either in its vault or in its account with the Federal Reserve. For an example of what happens when the reserve requirement for checking accounts is 10 percent, see Figure 6-3.

The bank takes 10 percent of your deposit and sets it aside. Now it has $900 in excess reserves ready to lend out. Someone comes in the door, borrows the $900 in the form of a $900 check, and deposits it in *his* bank, or spends it with a business, which then deposits it. Now another bank has $900 in new deposits. What do they do with it? They have to keep 10 percent

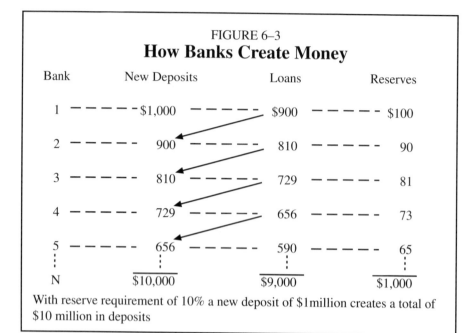

FIGURE 6–3
How Banks Create Money

Bank	New Deposits	Loans	Reserves
1	$1,000	$900	$100
2	900	810	90
3	810	729	81
4	729	656	73
5	656	590	65
⋮	⋮	⋮	⋮
N	$10,000	$9,000	$1,000

With reserve requirement of 10% a new deposit of $1million creates a total of $10 million in deposits

of their deposits on reserve but can loan out the rest. So they set aside $90 and loan out $810 to someone else, who then creates a new deposit in another bank, which has to keep 10 percent but can loan out the rest. By now you can see that the process has created new deposits in all banks that far exceed the original $1,000 deposit. One bank alone can't do it, but the banking system as a whole has created new money out of thin air, through an interesting system of creative accounting. That is called the **multiple expansion of bank deposits**, and that's where money comes from. That is the reason we earlier said there is something a bit mysterious about money. But that's how the system works and everyone benefits from it, not just the banks.

KEY CONCEPT

THE MULTIPLE EXPANSION OF BANK DEPOSITS IS THE PROCESS BY WHICH BANKS CREATE MONEY BY LOANING OUT DEPOSITS WHILE KEEPING A FRACTION OF THEM ON RESERVE.

How long can this process go on? That depends on the percentage of deposits that banks are required to keep on reserve. Since the amount that can be loaned gets smaller with each successive round, the process winds down faster if the reserve requirement is large, and it creates more money if it is small. With a 10 percent reserve requirement, as in the example, a deposit of $1,000 would end up as $10,000 of deposits—the original deposit plus $9,000 of new money. Now that you understand that, let's see how you can take advantage of the wide array of services that banks offer you.

WHAT BANKS DO

As you saw in the previous chapter, banks offer various types of checking and savings accounts, which are the safest forms of investment available. Commercial banks and savings and loan associations also offer many other services such as home mortgage loans, loans on the equity in your home, auto loans, loans on other purchases, and personal loans. Banks also make loans to businesses and help them finance their needs through inventory and other kinds of loans for cash flow and accounts receivable, for example. And, of course, they offer credit cards, which are a form of personal loans and a very handy thing to have, provided you use them carefully.

Probably the most important thing about dealing with a bank or other financial institution is establishing a personal relationship. If you are young, first open a checking account and use it responsibly, which means not over-drawing your account—bouncing checks. Then as you accumulate funds, open a savings account and use it to keep a small emergency fund, perhaps the 3 to 6 months income replacement most financial advisors suggest. Then you may be ready for a credit card, but you need to remember that most credit cards charge much more in interest than savings accounts pay. Clearly, it doesn't make sense to keep money in a savings account paying 3 percent while you are paying 13 percent for outstanding credit card balances.

A banker can also suggest ways to save for different financial goals or to pay debts. For example, often if an auto loan payment is deducted from a bank or checking account directly, the interest rate on the loan can be reduced slightly. Also, money can be deducted from bank accounts and moved to mutual funds or other investments on a regular basis. In any case, once you have established credit with a bank and, if possible, gotten to know your banker personally you will find a much friendlier reception when you want to take advantage of the other services banks offer, such as the home, auto or business loan you will probably want someday. Above all, *deal with your bank responsibly.* If you don't and you lose your credit rating, it can take a long time to get it back.

THE BIG PICTURE

Up to now you have been given the background necessary to develop a sound financial plan and secure a successful financial future. The only thing not yet discussed is how to understand the financial aspects of what's going on around you. That is, what's happening in the economy and how it can affect you. For example, you need to know if the economy is headed toward a recession that could cost you your job. You also need to know which way interest rates are heading so that you can plan your investment strategy accordingly, and much more. In other words, you need to know how to read the newspapers and especially the financial press, which often seems a complicated task, but in reality is not. All you need to know are a few basic things: how the government and the monetary authorities attempt to use fiscal and monetary policy to keep the economy on an even keel.

HOW THE ECONOMY WORKS

Some people say the economy works by itself, guided by competition and the laws of supply and demand. That's partly true, but there's a lot more to it than that. The government plays a large (too large, some say) and key role. Ever since Congress passed the Employment Act of 1946, the U.S. government has been charged with trying to keep the economy running as close to full employment as possible. How does the government go about doing that? It uses all the tools at its disposal to try to influence the levels of consumption, investment, government spending, exports and imports. These tools, which are used to control economic activity, fall into two distinct but related categories: fiscal policy and monetary policy.

Fiscal Policy

Fiscal policy is a catch-all phrase to describe how the government uses its powers of spending and taxing to influence the level of total production and hence, the level of employment and the rate of inflation. By increasing or decreasing government spending, the government can either create or eliminate jobs. The government can also affect the level of consumer and business spending by increasing or decreasing taxes, thereby reducing or raising the amount of after-tax income available to be spent.

```
KEY CONCEPT

FISCAL POLICY IS THE GOVERNMENT'S
ABILITY TO INFLUENCE THE LEVEL OF
ECONOMIC ACTIVITY BY INCREASING OR
DECREASING GOVERNMENT SPENDING
AND TAXES.
```

If the government wants to speed up the economy, it increases spending to create jobs and/or decreases taxes to increase private-sector spending. Likewise, if it wants to slow the economy down, it has two options. It can decrease its own spending or it can increase taxes. The latter course decreases the amount of after-tax income available to consumers and businesses.

Monetary Policy

Monetary policy in the United States is conducted by the Federal Reserve System (commonly called "the Fed"), which is the U.S. central bank that operates independently of Congress and the executive branch of government. Depending on its priorities, the Fed can increase the money supply, thereby giving banks more money to loan out, which stimulates investment and consumption. Or the Fed can decrease the money supply, which will make less money available for banks to lend, thereby slowing investment. The Fed can also decrease some key interest rates more directly, making borrowing cheaper and stimulating investment and consumer spending. Or it can raise interest rates and slow things down. With these tools the government and the central bank can accelerate economic activity or they can step on the brakes and slow the economy.

```
KEY CONCEPT

MONETARY POLICY IS THE CENTRAL BANK'S
ABILITY TO INFLUENCE ECONOMIC ACTIVITY BY
INCREASING OR DECREASING THE MONEY
SUPPLY AND CERTAIN KEY INTEREST RATES.
```

Of course, if it were all that simple, it wouldn't even need to be talked about. The problem is that using the monetary and fiscal policy tools to stimulate the economy does indeed create more jobs and spending. But it also—sooner or later—causes inflation. These tools can slow down the rate of inflation as well, but that usually causes the level of unemployment to rise. So, there tends to be a trade-off between inflation and unemployment, which muddies the waters and makes economics controversial because these are competing economic and political policy goals that affect different people in different ways.

The problem of managing the economy is a lot like fine tuning the engine of a car. It's a very delicate balancing act, and quite a bit more complex than we've made it look. However, if you understand the basic monetary and fiscal policy tools, and how they (are supposed to) work, you can understand what the government is trying to do and why. All this is summarized in Figure 6-4.

INJECTIONS—LEAKAGES APPROACH

Before continuing, let's see how the same process can be explained in a simpler way, one that is perhaps easier to understand. Let's consider the economy from the perspective of what goes into it that creates jobs and

---

FIGURE 6–4

The Basics of Fiscal and Monetary Policy

FISCAL POLICY

1. ↑↓Government Spending (G)
2. ↑↓Taxes (TX)

MONETARY POLICY (THE FED)

1. ↑↓The Money Supply (MS)
2. ↑↓Interest Rates (I)

IF INFLATION IS TOO HIGH:
↓G, ↑TX, ↓MS, ↑I

IF UNEMPLOYMENT IS TOO HIGH:
↑G, ↓TX, ↑MS, ↓I

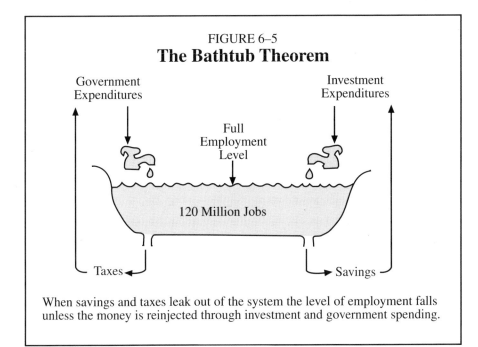

FIGURE 6–5
The Bathtub Theorem

Government Expenditures

Investment Expenditures

Full Employment Level

120 Million Jobs

Taxes

Savings

When savings and taxes leak out of the system the level of employment falls unless the money is reinjected through investment and government spending.

incomes (injections) compared to what leaks out of it that eliminates jobs and lowers the overall level of income (leakages).

Imagine that an economy is represented by a bathtub that you are looking at in cross section, as in Figure 6-5. The tub has two faucets and two drains. One faucet represents inflows of investment into the economy—the tub in this case. The other faucet represents government spending. As the water (G and I) flows into the tub, jobs are generated. Then try to imagine that the level of water in the tub represents a level of economic activity where there is less than full employment.

It's easy to see that if you add enough government spending and enough investment to the general level of consumption (economic activity) already going on in the tub, then you can bring the water level to full employment. As you have seen, this is one of the major macroeconomic goals. However, since the tub has two drains, one representing savings and one representing taxes, you can also see that not all of the added water will immediately increase the water level of economic activity.

Whenever savings are taken out of the economy (the tub), jobs are lost unless the savings are reinvested into the economy. By the same token, if taxes are taken out of income, less will be spent on consumption and jobs will be lost unless the government spends the tax revenues. If the savings and taxes are leaking out of the tub faster than the investment and government faucets are filling it, then the overall level of employment and economic activity will fall. That is, the water level will drop. On the other hand, if the consumption and investment faucets are pumping water—spending—into the tub faster than the tax and savings drains are letting it flow out, then the economy will have more jobs than it can handle, just as the tub will have more water than it can contain. People will be demanding more goods than the economy can produce, and the result will be inflation.

To keep the economy running at full employment, the government and the monetary authorities must constantly keep adjusting the faucets and the drains to achieve full employment without causing excessive inflation at the same time. This somewhat oversimplified way of looking at macroeconomics is, appropriately enough, called the "leakages and injections" approach to macroeconomic theory. Understanding this approach helps us comprehend the more complex models of the macroeconomy, and their variations.

If you understand these basic concepts, then you can understand what is happening when you see the newspaper headlines that say, for example: THE FED INCREASES INTEREST RATES. What does that mean? It means the Federal Reserve Board thinks the economy is doing too well for its own good and needs to be slowed down, lest inflation get out of hand and erode the value of everybody's savings. How does that affect you? In many ways. If you are a saver you will likely earn higher interest rates on your savings. But if you are a debtor you will likely have to pay higher rates of interest on your loans. And if you own bonds, look out, because their value is sure to fall. If you don't follow the economic and financial news to learn how it is going to affect you, then your ability to control your financial life will be severely limited. That won't happen to you, of course, because you have just read this book.

FIGURE 7–1 **Monthly Average Income**						
	MONTH	MONTH	MONTH	MONTH	MONTH	MONTH
Salary						
Invest. Income						
Bonuses						
Other						
Total Income:						
	MONTHLY AVERAGE EXPENSES					
TAXES						
Fed. Income						
FICA						
State & Local						
Other						
AUTO						
Gasoline						
Service						
Auto Loan						
Licenses						
Other						
HOUSING						
Rent						
Mortagage						
Electric						
Heat						
Water						
Telephone						
Other						
INSURANCE						
Auto						
Home						
Life						
Medical						
Disability						
Other						

FIGURE 7–1 (continued)
Monthly Average Income

	MONTH	MONTH	MONTH	MONTH	MONTH	MONTH
FOOD						
Groceries						
Restaurants						
School Lunches						
Other						
MISC.						
Clothing						
Entertainment						
Child Care						
Charity						
Bank Charges						
Credit card						
Gifts						
Education						
Home Repair						
Household						
Appliances						
Newspapers						
Magazines						
Other						
Total Expenses						
Inc. minus Exp.						

FIGURE 7–2 Net Worth Worksheet						
	MO/YR	MO/YR	MO/YR	MO/YR	MO/YR	MO/YR
ASSETS						
Investments						
Savings						
Checking						
Stock Mut. Funds						
Bond Mut. Funds						
*Life Ins.						
Money Market						
Cert. of Dep.						
Bonds						
Treasury Bonds						
Real Estate						
Individual Stocks						
Other						
Other						
Other						
OTHER ASSETS						
Vehicles						
Home						
Jewlery						
Furniture						
Other						
Other						
Other						
Other						
TOTAL ASSETS						

FIGURE 7–2 (continued)
Net Worth Worksheet

	MO/YR	MO/YR	MO/YR	MO/YR	MO/YR	MO/YR
LIABILITIES						
Mortgage						
Auto Loan						
Credit Card Bal.						
Other						
Other						
Other						
Other						
Other						
Other						
TOTAL LIABILITIES						
**NET WORTH						

   *   Cash value

 **   Assets minus liabilities

Index